40 Bites of Good

Because You Are What You Eat

LEWIS M. GREER

ISBN-13: 978-0-9993095-2-0 (Paperback edition)

ISBN-13: 978-0-9993095-9-9 (eBook edition)

Contents

Introduction

A lot of my work is done from my home office, which is also our primary library. Behind my chair are several reference books, placed where I can spin around, grab a bite of someone else's work and wisdom, then return to the task at hand.

Some of those books are utilitarian, like a dictionary and a thesaurus. Some are intended to be inspirational. If I need an idea, or to have my mind jostled, I grab one of those.

Two books are intentionally leaning, face forward, against the spines of other books that are shelved. One of those is *The Book of Virtues*, because it reminds me to write about good when I'm tempted to write about my own opinions.

The other is a small notebook, blank on the inside. It was a gift to me more than a decade ago from a young man who had just graduated from Stanford University with several prestigious academic awards.

On the white cover is a small drawing of Charlie Chaplin's famous character "the Tramp." Underneath the drawing are the words

I AM NOT
A BUM.
I AM
AN ARTIST.

I hope Joseph (the giver) believed that of me. I hope he still believes it. I work very hard to make it true.

My art is not with a brush and paints, it is with words. Each week I write more than 1,000 of them in the form of an article that will appear on the Do Good U website. That schedule both frees me to write and forces me to write, and I know it is an art because I desire both.

There are two things all writers do: they write, and they read. There are two things all writers want: to write something useful, and to write something accessible. That is, the writer wants the readers (or listeners) to find themselves in the words.

My hope is that *40 Bites of Good. Because you are what you eat,* will be both useful and nourishing. I hope you can see yourself in some of these articles, and I hope you will allow the words to get into you and feed your mind and soul with good.

Each article, you may have already guessed, was written originally for posting on the Do Good U website.

Some articles, therefore, will contain references to something happening at the time of writing. For instance, the global pandemic (COVID-19) was a natural thing to write about. You may or may not have been impacted by it directly, but like a reader who has never been in battle reading about a war, you will still understand it.

A word or two about the title. When I grab a reference book, especially a thesaurus, I cannot resist grabbing an extra bite or two from it. Like a thesaurus, *40 Bites* is not intended to be eaten all at once. Of course it is certainly fine to have more than one bite at a time.

My friend Erik suggested a phrase that led directly to the subtitle, and I think it is perfect. "You are what you eat" was first coined in 1826 by a French lawyer, but it didn't become popular around the world until it was used in America a hundred years later.

It was never about actual food, though. It was about what you put into your mind and your heart and your soul, and it still is.

At Do Good U, our goal is to bring more good into the world. My hope is that as you get more "good" into you through this book, you will be an agent of good in every part of your life. Our hope and prayer is that your family, your friends, your co-workers will all be the beneficiaries of you consuming these words.

Enjoy the bites, and do good. It's in you.

Chapter 1

Is It Really Good?

When we first started Do Good University, people asked what we would do.

"Help people learn to do good," we would say, and that was often followed by the question, "What is good?"

As it turns out, that's a good (no pun intended) question.

Because there are different kinds of good, let's make sure we are talking about the same good.

First, there is the kind of good that is about quality. It's the "Good" you would use when the restaurant server comes up to your table, timing it perfectly to make sure your mouth is full, and asks, "How is everything?"

You know that server, obviously a professional, is inwardly smiling at your attempt to answer the question as you try to swallow the very large bite of the sandwich you just shoved in with both hands.

"Guhd," you mumble out, while also trying to hold that slippery piece of avocado hostage.

And by "good" you mean the quality of the food is acceptable. It is possible, though, that you meant the food was enjoyable. "This is good!" And that's another kind of good.

There are still other kinds of good, but the one we focus on at Do Good U is *possessing or displaying moral virtue*. A good person, a good deed. Sometimes even a good reputation.

Kinds and Degrees

You'll notice I've been talking about different *kinds* of good. When things are in fact different, they are different in one of two ways. They are different in kind, or they are different in degree.

If one house is larger than another, they are different in degree. A car and a house, however, are different in kind. Carpet and tile may both be used for flooring, but they are also different in kind.

If someone gives a gift of $1 to a nonprofit and someone else gives $1,000,000 to the same nonprofit, the gifts are different only in degree.

When things are different in degree, there can always be intermediates — for instance gifts that are between $1 and $1,000,000. If they are different in kind, there can be no intermediates.

And thus ends Philosophy 101 in the differences between things. Give yourself an A+, which is different in degree from a B-.

Judging moral goods

As I said, at Do Good U we are focused on moral good. Yes, we believe in and value high quality. Moral good, though, is different in kind from qualitative good. The finest diamond in the world has no moral value.

I have a young friend who taught fifth grade. If my fifth grade teacher had been as nice as this young woman is, I would have purposely failed fifth grade so I could repeat it.

So when I first learned that she didn't have a boyfriend, I was like, "What?!" Then I told her that I wasn't going to try to fix her up, as I imagined many were doing, but instead I would pray that God would send along exactly the right guy.

She appreciated that, then said, "Just make sure he's a good guy."

Isn't that cool? She didn't say rich, or handsome, she said "good."

Good for her. But how will she know?

How *do* you know?

Knowing whether or not someone is good is a matter of discernment. The way my friend said, "make sure he's a good guy" told me she had already figured out there were "not good" guys out there.

Such was the case for some very savvy investors. The headline for the article in the July 2, 2021 Wall Street Journal caught my eye: *He Convinced the Elite He Invested for Good. Then the Money Vanished.*

The article was adapted from a book, published by Harper Business and titled *The Key Man: The True Story of How the Global Elite Was Duped by a Capitalist Fairy Tale.*

My point is not to cast aspersions on the global elite. Suffice it to say you would know by name many of those who together invested more than $1 billion dollars into a company that claimed it was going to harness capitalism and use it for good. And almost none of those sophisticated investors and famous people suspected it was a lie.

On a "closer to home" note, a friend of a friend had her house stolen from her by con artists just a few years ago. They convinced her she owed money to the IRS (she did not) and that the IRS was going to take her home — her largest asset — to settle her debt. But she could protect her home by signing it over to their nonprofit, and so she did.

Those people were apparently good but not really good. Unless you mean really good at being evil.

Being a good person isn't about being good on the outside, it's about being good from the inside out

Real and apparent good

An apparent good is that which people assume is to their benefit and is something they desire, but in fact it is not to their benefit. A real good is something that is to their benefit and something they should desire even if they do not desire it.

Now that you know that, will you be able to discern between real and apparent goods (including people) on a moral level? I hope knowing there are different kinds of good, that moral good is the highest kind, and that some goods aren't real, will help.

There are still challenges, though, many of which come from "the loudest voice" syndrome. For instance, is teaching Critical Race Theory in schools a real or an apparent good? My personal examination says it is not a real good. Your answer may differ. Either way, you can see that thought is required.

As for answering the restaurant server while you are still swallowing, just smile with your eyes and nod. After all, you know it's not good to talk with your mouth full.

Do good. It's in you. Really.

Chapter 2

How to Be happy

N o, that headline is not click bait. Happiness is available to every person, including you. In fact the Declaration of Independence says that happiness is your right.

In these days of so many individuals declaring their own self-interested rights, the historic document takes us to far greater heights.

The second paragraph in the Declaration begins:

We hold these Truths to be self-evident, that all Men are created equal, that they are endowed by their Creator with certain unalienable Rights, that among these are Life, Liberty, and the Pursuit of Happiness.

And there it is: all people have a right to live, a right to be free, and a right to happiness. Those rights are "unalienable," which means they cannot be taken away from the holder.

"But wait," you might be thinking. "It says *the pursuit of happiness.*" It does indeed, and to many today that sounds like this. "You have the right to *go after* happiness."

However *pursuit* in 1776, especially here, meant "achieve" rather than "chase."

Arthur Schlesinger Jr., a historian and son of a historian, pointed that out back in the 1960's. His study answered my question about why I had a right to life and liberty, but only the right to "pursue" (in the modern definition) happiness.

But it did not answer my other question about the phrase, which is a little more challenging: What is happiness?

Defining Happiness

Dictionaries will tell you that *happiness* is "the state of being happy," then go on to say that *happy* is "feeling or showing pleasure or contentment."

That is the happy of *Don't Worry, Be Happy*. It is the happy of Happy Birthday. Whether or not it is the happy of *Happy Gilmore* is an interesting question.

But it is not the happy of the Declaration of Independence.

I don't mean to dismiss pleasure or contentment. They are important. For now, though, let us turn the pages of something other than a dictionary to find a deeper meaning of happiness.

You won't be surprised to hear that great thinkers going back thousands of years considered the topic of happiness. Even Jesus had some quite profound and surprising things to say about it.

Did those thinkers all agree on what happiness was? For the most part they did! Here is a fun test that might help you understand their conclusion. *Complete this sentence: I want to be happy because*
-------------------.

And the survey says...

OK, that was a trick question. There is no "because," and the simple reason is that being happy is the end goal. As Mortimer J. Adler said, "Happiness is the ultimate good that everyone seeks."

Now we are getting somewhere! Happiness is not a feeling, it is a state of being. Rich people and poor people alike are sometimes happy people. Sick people and healthy people are also both often happy. Circumstances, which are mostly beyond our control, are not the determining factor in happiness.

Even though both the rich and poor can be and are happy, we still persist in thinking, "If I just had a little more money I would be happy."

Here's an interesting insight for you: even the very rich say that!

Money really cannot buy you happiness. It can certainly buy you pleasure, at least for a moment. Ask any user of cocaine how that felt the first time, and how they chased it, and how much it cost them.

Even if we all want pleasure, it is not "the ultimate good that everyone seeks."

Good and happy

If you think philosophers have spent a lot of time on the topic of happiness, you should see how much effort they have put into good! Often this shows up as "good and evil," because sometimes it makes sense to think about them together.

For now, though, let good (after all, we are Do Good U) be our focus. Here's a story to help.

Imagine you are invited to meet with four very special benefactors, each of whom promises to make your life good.

Naturally, you go.

The first benefactor you meet is an impeccably dressed man. "I can give you wealth," he says, "and all that comes with it. All you have to do is give me most of your time and attention, and keep me uppermost in your mind."

Next is a very fit, very beautiful woman. She says, "I can give you excellent health, strength and good looks. Just spend most of your time with me and keep me first in your thoughts."

Benefactor three is a hip young man carrying two phones. He snaps your pic and does something with it. "I've already started making you socially famous," he says. "That post will have a million views, and we can get many more. It takes time, of course, so remember to bring me into everything you do."

The final benefactor is a woman who almost glows with serenity. Her gifts, she says, are wisdom and the moral virtues. You ask her, "Do I need to spend all my time with you?"

"In a way," she answers. "If you truly want my gifts we can't have a casual relationship. I need to live in you."

"And if I do," she continues, "you can have all those other goods with far less effort, because I will help you get them in the right ways and in the right amounts."

Which benefactor will you choose?

One last insight before you decide. Only the goods of wisdom and virtue are completely in your control. The goods of wealth, health, and even friendship often depend on chance.

How to be happy

Philosophers and theologians agree on this: the "soul goods" of the virtues and wisdom are desired naturally. Without them we feel that something is missing, and true happiness is not possible -- even if we possess the lesser (but useful) goods of wealth, health, and social standing in abundance.

Let wisdom, courage, honesty, humility, love, faith and the other virtues live in your soul, and you will find real happiness.

Do good. Be happy. It's in you!

Chapter 3

What If No One Was Watching You?

Recently I asked a young friend a question. "You've played tournament golf at a very high level. What have you learned?"

Without hesitating he said, "I've learned that no one is watching me."

I knew exactly what he meant. Pretty much everyone who has played in a tournament (basketball, tennis, golf, etc.) has felt the pressure of everyone's eyes on them, even if they weren't.

My friend was saying he finally figured out it wasn't about him. Yes, his family and friends in the crowd were watching. His fellow competitors (as they are known in golf tournaments) watched to ensure the rules were kept and the score was correctly reported. Other than that, only God was watching. And none of those -- friends, competitors, or even God -- was going to judge him for hitting either good or bad shots.

For some of us, that's hard to learn. I once played in a golf event where I had to hit a shot on a par three with 4 professionals and 11 other amateurs standing on the tee. And watching, I thought.

I wish I'd know then that none of them were really watching me. At the time I felt every eye looking for flaws to critique.

It was too bad for them that they weren't watching, because I hit a great shot. For the day, as it turned out, mine was the closest to the hole.

No eyes

P. G. Wodehouse wrote: "*Golf... is the infallible test. The man who can go into a patch of rough alone, with the knowledge that only God is watching him, and play his ball where it lies, is the man who will serve you faithfully and well.*"

I imagine the same would be true for many (most?) people driving a car if "only God" was watching. How would you drive if you had a twenty mile stretch of "enforcement free" road? Faster than the speed limit, I'm guessing.

Thieves generally work in the dark, either literally or figuratively. Their goal is to not be seen. They want to avoid having eyes on them, so they use the "cover of darkness." If you could cloak yourself with invisibility, how would you behave? Would you use that power to go places you wouldn't otherwise go? Would you use it to steal?

You may have noticed that the examples I've given are negative. I didn't ask, for instance, if you would go around doing good deeds unseen if you could be invisible. A real life tooth fairy, perhaps?

That would be amazing, and it's fun to ponder the possibilities. (If you think of one, let me know.)

Aside from positive behavior changes, which I'm coming back to, there is something else to consider about being watched.

We all want to be seen.

See me

I don't mean we all want to be in "the public eye." That can get overwhelming. Just ask Tiger Woods, who named his yacht *Privacy* and uses it primarily to get away from people. Adding to the privacy, he takes it out to sea and SCUBA dives.

We may not want to be famous, but have you ever noticed people at sporting events when they are on the JumboTron? When people see themselves being seen on the big screen, they often get a little silly. If they've recorded the event they send that clip to their friends. Maybe you've done that.

I'm not a psychologist, but in my experience knowing we are seen creates a connection. It might be brief, but it is real. So here is a tip for you if you happen to notice anyone on the street who is truly homeless. *Look at them so they know they are seen.*

Even people standing on a corner with a sign asking for money (they are probably not homeless, regardless of what their sign might say) can get a lot out of eye contact and a nod of the head. And doing that might be good for you, too.

Being seen can take different forms. Having your work acknowledged is being seen. Someone holding a door for you means you've been seen. It doesn't take a lot of effort to see people, but it does require intent.

Being seen -- or watched -- changes our behavior for the better

One of the most intense places to work, I understand, is in an operating room where critical surgeries are performed.

A life can sometimes be on the line, time is often a challenge, mistakes can have terrible consequences, and every person working there is literally an expert. Leadership in the OR is different than outside it. Someone who is a peer outside might be the boss inside, so communication can be challenging.

In Australia, a "three-month experiment was undertaken to address a widespread culture of bullying and poor behaviour in surgical theatres." (Notice the Australian spelling? These findings were published by the University of South Australia.)

They tried "*a novel experiment to address offensive and rude comments in operating theatres by placing 'eye' signage in surgical rooms.*

The eye images, attached to the walls of an Adelaide orthopaedic hospital's operating theatre without any explanation, had the desired effect in markedly reducing poor behaviour among surgical teams."

The lead researcher, Professor Cheri Ostroff, "attributed the result to a perception of being "watched," even though the eyes were not real." Amazing!

Some think those who "watch" are there to judge them, whether for good or ill. Generally we try to please watchers.

Some think of "being seen" as an acknowledgement of their existence, which is powerful.

However you define them, know that both being watched and being seen will almost always improve your behavior for the better.

Knowing that, you can do a great deal of good by *seeing* other people, and, in an appropriate time and manner, *watching* them.

If you ever feel unwatched or unseen, remember that God is always watching you, and he always sees you. Even when you are SCUBA diving.

Do good. It's in you, and people see it.

Chapter 4

We Should Remember, and Here's Why

I f you've flown on a commercial airline in the last couple of decades, you've heard these words: "May I have your attention, please?"

For many passengers, the answer appears to be "No."

Newer flyers usually do pay attention. Those who have flown often, like me, watch to see how well the flight attendant performs the unenviable task of the safety briefing. Road warriors don't even look up.

The airlines know all that. Sometimes they add, "Even if you fly frequently..." for those of us who give less attention to the flight attendant than we should. Over the years I've seen the airlines try a number of things to get us to pay attention. They've used videos (some very well done), they've used humor (Southwest, primarily), and they have been very serious.

I have yet to see an airline use a Catholic nun carrying a wooden ruler, but I'm thinking that might help.

Why do they ask for your attention? Because without you giving it, you are highly unlikely to remember anything about safety.

Attention is a fundamental element in remembering things, from the main point of a sermon to the name of that person you met five minutes ago.

There are other factors in remembering things, to be sure, but attention is a biggie. A few years ago, after a series of flights, I was sure I could deliver a safety briefing myself. I was wrong, so now I pay attention. Just in case.

Intention

How do you give attention? You have done it, so you can. There have been other times when you failed to do it. The best way, perhaps, to give attention is to be intentional about it.

Here is how *not* to do that, because, you know, I want to help.

You are not intentional about paying attention when you *invite* distractions. For instance, you are having coffee with a friend who needs your advice. You sit down at a table with your drinks, and you pull your phone out of your pocket and place it face up on the table, where you can see it at a glance.

What are the odds that you will receive a notification of some kind during your conversation? Yep, 100%. And not only will you look at your phone, you will pick it up and look carefully. Where is your attention? Not on your friend.

Does your friend care? Maybe not, but what your actions say is, "I care about me more than I care about you."

We have all been guilty of inviting distractions, or, on a slightly less offensive level, failing to block distractions.

About 30 minutes ago I was writing away on this article. I was focused and paying attention to writing about paying attention. My phone was sitting in its charger, facing me. Suddenly it lit up and let me know a text had arrived. I picked up the phone, saw that the text was spam, deleted it, and then looked at an earlier text. A second spam text arrived, this one with pictures. I deleted it and reported it as spam. Then came a third spam text from the same source, asking if I got the pictures. Delete. Report.

Now safe again, I still held the phone in my hands. A game of sudoku somehow opened and was played. I looked out the window and thought something in the back yard could use my attention. Time passed, and words were not written.

It was not my intention to create an illustration about how not to pay attention, but it's nice when something good comes out of my own failures.

Now my phone is on "Do Not Disturb," and I am intentionally paying attention to what I'm writing.

Remember this

The idea of writing about "remembering" occurred to me on Memorial Day. It is a day of remembrance, specifically remembering those in the military who gave their lives in the line of duty. My wife and I watched the Memorial Day Concert, which always has great stories to help us remember that America is truly "the land of the free because of the brave."

That gives us an important reason to remember: we are the beneficiaries of the sacrifices of men and women decades -- even centuries -- ago. If we fail to remember, we not only do a disservice to those who came before us, we deeply diminish our appreciation for the blessings we enjoy.

It isn't just Memorial Day when we remember. On July 4, we remember that the United States was once "the colonies," and subject to Great Britain, but with intent and sacrifice gained independence. Every Christmas we are reminded that God sent his son to be born as a baby and live as a man on earth.

Easter reminds us that Jesus, that same son of God, was raised from the dead and still lives. A cross reminds us of that as well.

Without these reminders, are we likely to forget? Apparently we are.

My reason for saying so is simple: in the Bible God told people over and over (and over), "Remember." In fact it would be a fascinating study to look at the use of the word throughout the Bible. One use is consistent: God says he *will* remember, and I believe it. Likewise he tells us we *need to* remember, knowing we are prone to forget, and I believe that, too.

According to a fascinating book called *Why We Remember*, "Memory does more than store knowledge or keep track of what we've seen, it points to what we can and should do in the future."

I love things that help us remember, like statues and plaques and paintings. I love storytellers and docents. Books, from history to autobiography, are among my favorites.

Books often recount the evil men have done, and we need to remember those deeds as well. They point us to what we should never repeat or allow in the future.

May our memories point us toward doing more and more good, and may future generations remember us for that.

Remember to do good. It's in you.

Chapter 5

The Future of America

You may not feel the need for an article like this. (*Note: this was written in late October, 2024, just a few days before a national presidential election.*) It could be that you have decided not to vote at all in this election, which is just over two weeks away. Or it could be that you've decided how you'll vote and nothing will change your mind.

But in the not-too-distant-future, the opportunity to change your mind about whether or how to vote will be gone. So allow me to ask for a few minutes of your time to consider some things.

It should be no surprise that "doing good" will be at the heart of this. You undoubtedly like the idea of doing good and in fact do good often. On behalf of the world, thank you for that.

Of course now and then there are differences of opinion about what is good and what is evil. In cases like that, there has to be an outside -- and ideally objective -- standard to which we can appeal.

Finally, we also use these two phrases, and they might come into play in an election: *The greater good* and *The lesser of two evils.*

Vote

No matter who or what you vote for (candidates and propositions), please vote.

Every election, even in America's quadrennial presidential elections, there are millions of registered voters who don't vote. In the last presidential election (2020), about 75 million registered voters did not vote.

Here's a quote on that from an Associated Press article:

According to a study by the Center for Inclusive Democracy at the University of Southern California, more than 75 million people eligible to vote — including nearly 35 million Black, Hispanic and Asian American people — did not cast ballots in the 2020 presidential election.

The positive number, though, was that even with those missing votes, the voting-eligible people who did cast a ballot was the highest in decades!

Being able to vote and not voting is not evil, but it's a failure to do good. It is a failure to speak into the life and culture of America, or to stand for your position on an issue.

The AP article also reveals why some people don't vote. Some have a personal reason not to vote (*e.g.* they don't like either candidate), and some can't navigate the process. There are those who think their vote doesn't matter.

For me, the higher the vote count, the more I think the will of the nation is being heard. The bigger the number, the easier I feel about the results. So please, if you can, vote. It'll make me feel better.

Leadership

One topic I haven't heard much about in this election is leadership.

You might not have noticed that it was missing, what with all the talk about this or that issue. I get that, because the issues (next section) appeal to our emotions, and we love living in our emotions.

But here at Do Good U we think about leadership a lot. In fact schools and businesses regularly engage us to teach leadership. We work with executives, students, and everyone in between, because leadership is a big deal.

Coach K (the famous Mike Krzyzewski, with 16 championships and 6 gold medals), says, "I think leadership is the least taught occupation that there is in the world, but it's the occupation that transcends every occupation."

Leadership is far from being the least written about occupation. In our Do Good library we have dozens of books on leadership. I can't imagine how many articles we have. But we agree with Coach K, leadership is rarely taught, even though it is transcendent in its importance.

So, among the candidates you'll be voting for, who is a leader worthy of your followership?

One of the characteristics of true leaders is this: they have a vision for the future and can articulate it. No vision, no leadership. That is the kind of thing we did as teenagers. "Let's all get together and go somewhere and do something." It's a crowd, not a leader with followers.

Every leader leads in context. A battlefield leader may have different skills than the president of a nonprofit ministry. Coaches of grade school athletes might have different personalities than professional coaches.

Effective leaders aren't always liked, but they always lead the way. Follow anyway, if that leader is going where you want to go.

Issues

OK, get your opinions out, but don't leave your mind behind.

On the national and state level there are several issues to

consider. The biggie for me is abortion, but the biggie for you may be the border, or foreign relations, or the economy.

A lot of the election ads are about those issues, and that's understandable. Issues are important, and what we do with some of these issues might well outlive those who get elected.

Here is what I'd like for you to do with all of the issues you can think of in this election:

Ask yourself which side of that issue is good, and which side is evil. Then support the good.

The challenge is that good and evil are not always crystal clear. Christians will tell you that is because Satan (evil) himself often appears as an angel of light. In other words, things that are evil are made to look good.

When it comes to abortion, I get that there are cases when it is necessary -- though still sad -- to end the life of an unborn child. It was Bill Clinton who said (in 1992) that abortion should be "safe, legal, and rare." In her own presidential campaign in 2008, Hillary Clinton echoed that and said, "and by rare, I mean *rare*." At this year's DNC, she dropped the "rare" part altogether.

Some say it is a moral good for a mother to be able to choose to end the life of her child. Mother Teresa said, "If a mother can kill her own children, then what can be next?"

Here is a choice for us all: to stand with good and against evil. Sometimes that choice is very, very difficult. Even then, choose good and do good.

It's in you.

Chapter 6

Garbage Collectors

My wife and I were in Hawaii on vacation. It's a place we both love for its beauty, its feel, and its people.

Kauai is our most frequent destination there, and we know it fairly well. We frequent local restaurants, but it can be challenging to find iced tea with extra ice, the way my wife likes it. So one day we stopped at a McDonald's for tea.

After we sat for a bit I got up and headed to the restroom. I passed by a Hawaiian gentleman sitting alone at a table. I nodded to him, but then got stopped at the door by a sign saying I needed a key. As I turned back toward the counter the fellow said, "No key. Pull hard."

Without a word I turned back, grabbed the handle, pulled hard, and sure enough the door opened. "Mahalo," I said, and on my way back to our table I stopped to chat with him. With genuine joy he told me he was going to heaven soon. He was 90, and he was excited.

Talk story

Soon my wife headed to the restroom and I said, "No key. Just pull hard." The man smiled, and my wife joined us a few minutes later.

That locked door opened a brief but delightful friendship for us. The man could "talk story!" He had, after all, been the head of the roads department for the Island of Kauai for more than 20 years and had worked on the roads for more than 40.

But it was a story about his son that stuck with us. "He is very smart," said the father, "so he became a garbage collector."

"What my son did," the dad explained, "was look and see what everybody needed and nobody wanted to do." Soon he added cleaning septic tanks to his business, along with other "dirty" work. Some months, we were told, he made a year's worth of income!

The Bad Kind

You may be a professional garbage collector — the good kind. But all of us are garbage collectors, even if we don't realize it. I know that because we are on the internet, which can be a filthy place.

Newspapers once had gossip columnists who wrote about "the swells" and who had attended which parties. At least they were called "gossip columns," so they could be read with that filter in mind.

Now gossip is called "breaking news," which often is less accurate than the gossip columns of old. The stories almost always lean to the bad, the headlines are written not to inform but to ensnare, and the content is rarely worth our time.

A lot of what is out there is just plain garbage.

Do we get rid of it? Not us. We suck in the garbage (character assassination, name calling, fear mongering, etc.), let it fester inside us, and then we spread it around to unsuspecting people known as friends and family.

If it is really tasty garbage, we save those morsels for our friends who like the high-octane stuff. We regurgitate what we've heard and feed each other, growing the garbage pile even higher.

Where does the garbage go?

That kind of garbage goes first to your mind, but eventually ends up in your heart. On this very day as I write, I can tell you there a lot of people whose hearts are less healthy than they were last year.

Talking with two friends today, and in fact both were saying they had a kind of malaise and had been dealing with it for a few months. They were both glad the three of us were together because it was a "positive" thing that helped alleviate those bad feelings.

We want to blame our damaged hearts on the pandemic and the election and the division in the political parties. Those things are not the problem, we are.

Yes, some of our intake is passive. When you are out in the world you are going to get germs on your hands and garbage in your heart. Just don't let either of those take root. Wash your hands, and if you are going to actively ingest garbage, get rid of it as soon as you can.

Make the switch

If you switch to a whole foods plant-based diet for your health, you will face a few days of withdrawal from the foods you were eating. But in a fairly short time you will miss those things less. Soon your tastes will change, and you'll actually desire healthy food.

I know this for a fact because I sort of switched to a whole foods plant-based diet. That is to say, my wife switched. I'm not as careful about it as she is, or as committed. But when I heard myself tell her one evening that I wanted a salad for dinner instead of a hamburger, I knew something had changed.

The same thing can happen to you with what you watch on TV,

with what you read, and with whom you associate. (That includes your favorite talk show hosts and newscasters.)

Notice that I'm advocating a switch, not a "stop cold turkey" approach. We need interaction with others, we want to be informed, and we need to grow.

Three steps to better health

First, change your "diet" to make it heart healthier. "Original programming" is a dangerous phrase when streaming movies or TV, for instance. It's like reading the labels on food you buy. Learn to be careful with your intake.

Second, make sure you receive a lot of positive input. Read great literature, read the Bible, watch uplifting movies with happy endings, and hang out with people who are wise. In fact the Bible has a book of wisdom (Proverbs), which includes this verse: *Walk with the wise and become wise, for a companion of fools suffers harm.*

Third, stop sharing garbage with others. We all covered our mouths with masks to stop the possible spread of COVID-19. How about if we just keep our mouths shut to stop the certain spread of garbage to other people's hearts?

Let's be the good kind of garbage collectors and dispose of all that trash in a healthy and responsible way. I guarantee that every one of us who does that will be doing good and making the world a better place to live.

Do good. It's in you!

Chapter 7

Those Who Call Evil Good and Good Evil

Have you ever tried to help someone and been smacked down for it?

If you are older than about 20, the answer is probably yes. It could be something as innocuous as holding a door open for someone (a classic -- and classy -- do good move), and then having the person say, in kind of a mean sounding way, "I can get my own door."

If that sounds like a made-up story, it's only because it's hard to imagine, but it happened to me once. I got over it immediately, but it was kind of a shock.

A big part of this whole "do good" thing, as you know, is that you don't do it for the reward. Rewards ("Thank you!") are nice and enjoyable and reinforce doing good. We all like them. But they are not *the* reason.

Recently a new friend, who happens to be in the book business, learned that I was writing a book. He asked, "If you knew you wouldn't sell a single copy of this book, would you still write it?" Well, yes.

If you knew you weren't going to be praised or even recognized for doing something good, would you still do it?

What if you knew you were going to be criticized?

The desire for "outside" approval can be -- and I think is -- one of the biggest challenges of the social media age. If we don't get followers, or clicks, or likes, or retweets, we feel like we have failed.

Allow me to clarify one thing: there is a difference in *making a living on* the approval of others and *living on* the approval of others. The first is fine, and a lot of people do it. The second is dangerous, and I do not recommend it.

How far would you go?

All of us like approval. Most of us are confident enough and wise enough to know when to draw the line in seeking it. Some are not.

It is only speculation, so please take it as that, but I can imagine that Thomas Matthew Crooks thought he would be famous if he assassinated Mr. Trump. Perhaps he believed he was doing good.

The same is true of another "assassin," of sorts. A man named Judas Iscariot.

There are plenty of assassinations in the Bible -- this was technically not one of them, but it was close enough to count. Judas had been a follower of Jesus for around three years. At some point in his life, Judas left behind what he had and joined with a rag-tag group of young men who walked with, ate with, and learned from Jesus.

Jesus and Judas didn't always agree. One area they differed on was the use of the small amount of money they had. Judas had an informed opinion about that topic, because he was the treasurer.

Justification and wisdom

When he finally decided that he would betray Jesus, his question to the authorities was, "How much will you pay me?" Judas was paid 30 pieces of silver -- perhaps $400 in today's wages, though the value is not really relevant. Money, in this case, was used only as a justification for an action Judas had been thinking about for a while.

Apparently some assumed reward, whether it was only fame or also fortune, was in the mind of young Mr. Crooks. He did not see it, dying within seconds of his opening act.

As for Judas, he lived to see that his act was evil, and he tried to reverse it. He tried to give back the money and said, "I have sinned by betraying innocent blood." Refused by those he thought were on his side, Judas ended his own life.

When you find yourself justifying some action of yours you think is good, think again. Good is its own reward and does not need to be justified.

It doesn't seem like it would be that difficult to recognize the justification of our own actions, but a lot of people miss it. Judas missed it. But once the action is taken, justifications melt away. They are no longer of any use except to remind us of our guilt.

What it takes to decide whether an act is truly good is simple wisdom. It does not require a great deal of deliberation, it requires reflection. Of course the more good you do, the more you know good from evil.

While it is possible for people to take the good you do and spurn it, always choose good. Never, ever, do evil while calling it good.

A warning

Isaiah was a prophet who, inspired by God, wrote these words about 2,700 years ago:

> Woe to those who call evil good
> and good evil,
> who put darkness for light
> and light for darkness,
> who put bitter for sweet
> and sweet for bitter!

Woe to those who are wise in their own eyes,
and shrewd in their own sight!

The other way around

Joseph was the 11th son of Jacob, the grandson of Abraham. He was Jacob's favorite, in large part because he was the first son of Rachel, the love of Jacob's life.

His brothers sold him into slavery in Egypt, where, 13 years later, they came to buy food. Joseph saw them, treated them kindly, and eventually brought the entire family of Jacob (also called Israel) to Egypt. When Jacob died the brothers assumed Joseph would now kill them, and they finally asked for Joseph's forgiveness.

Here is my favorite part: Joseph said to them, "You meant it for evil, but God meant it for good."

Isn't that amazing? God, who loves good, took an evil act and turned it into good: Joseph, sold into slavery, saved not only Egypt but the entire family of Israel. That family became the nation of Israel.

Judas did evil, and God turned that into the greatest good ever.

But don't put God to the test. Never do evil. Always do good. It's in you.

Chapter 8

Who Do You Trust?

I don't know if there are still daredevils around. I do know there is a Marvel character called Daredevil ("real" name Matt Murdock), and I even know *Daredevil: Born Again* will air on Disney+ sometime in 2025.

What I'm wondering about is people like Evel Knievel and Karl Wallenda and Philippe Petit. In case you don't know any of those, they all performed feats of daring for public entertainment. Of the three, Knievel is the best known and Petit is the most recent. He's also the only one still living.

Knievel is remembered primarily for jumping motorcycles over long distances. There was a lot of talk about the Grand Canyon, but that never happened. And he failed to jump the fountains at Caesar's Palace, but he tried. He was badly injured in that one. Along the way he did break a lot of records, and also a lot of bones. But he was the real deal.

In 1974, at the age of 25 or so, Philippe Petit walked on a wire between The World Trade Center twin towers. Everything about that feat was incredible, including the fact of getting the wire installed (clandestinely) 1,350 feet above the ground.

29

A documentary made in 2008 about his performance won an Oscar, so you know the story is great. He had the idea when he was just 18 and happened to see an article about the building of the towers. He finished the show in the rain.

Karl Wallenda was also a high-wire artist. At 65, Wallenda walked on a wire 1/4 mile across Tallulah Gorge in Georgia. He did two headstands along the way.

A thrill ride

But the rope walker daredevil of them all, in many ways, was Charles Blondin. He was the first person to cross Niagara Falls on a tight rope, which he did on June 30, 1859. He did it again on July 4 (Independence Day) and on July 14 (Bastille Day -- Blondin was in fact Frenchman Jean-François Gravelet).

Blondin continued to cross the 1,100 foot distance on the 3.24 inch rope, 100 feet above the water, over the next several weeks. He did it blindfolded, on stilts, and once while pushing a wheelbarrow carrying a stove. That time he stopped in the middle and cooked an omelet, ate it, and continued on.

In the greatest crossing, though, he carried a man on his back.

He offered a reward for anyone who would ride with him. No one took it. Blondin's manager and best friend ultimately did. He couldn't let his friend down, and he hoped his friend would not let him "down" either.

The crossing was anything but easy. Each man weighed 140 pounds. The balancing pole weighed 45 pounds. It was very hard work. But obviously they made it, or Blondin would be far less famous.

There are several important lessons in all this, but the one I'd like us to focus on is trust.

All those people, even for a reward, would not trust Charles Blondin with their life. Did they believe he could carry them safely across? Many probably did, but their trust did not overcome their fear.

Would I have hopped on his back? Would you? "Who do you trust" suddenly becomes a serious question.

The lesson. And the other part of it.

There are several videos about Charles Blondin carrying Harry Colcord (that was his name) on his back across the falls. The lesson that is almost always taken from that -- and it is a good one -- is, "Who do you trust to carry you across?"

That might be across the falls, across the finish line, or across the chasm from earth to heaven.

We trust other people (to some degree) every time we get on the road with them. We trust barbers, butchers, and bankers. Of course we trust doctors and nurses and police officers. That last group we might trust with our lives, as we do airline pilots and the mechanics who inspected the plane.

But that is only part of the lesson. The other part of the lesson is this: *Who trusts you?*

Only Harry Colcord trusted Charles Blondin. But Charles also trusted Harry. It took a mutual trust for that walk to work. Blondin told his passenger, "Don't try to balance, and keep looking up."

All of us are well versed in trusting others. We practice it a lot, generally without giving it much thought.

But who trusts you? How do you make yourself trustworthy, and how often do you offer to carry someone on your back over a dangerous path?

To begin with a simple question, are you trustworthy?

Entrust

Sometimes I describe myself as a "geek wannabe."

I worked in a high-tech company for several years, and I loved living in geekdom. So I kind of still pay attention to technology, especially in networking.

Recently I noticed an article that said Google and Firefox would no longer trust Entrust. What does that mean? Entrust is one of many companies that make software which is supposed to make web sites (in particular) and other internet communications secure. Part of that is called SSL/TLS. If a website address begins with https as opposed to http, it is secured through an SSL certificate.

The Entrust name implies that they should be trusted. Now they are not.

Neither naming yourself Entrust nor saying, "Trust me!" makes you trustworthy. So what does?

In some cases trust is about ability. The tightrope walker, for instance, or a hair stylist or a chef. Sometimes it is about strength. But most of the time trust is about honesty and reliability.

If you want to be trustworthy, tell the truth.

Condoleezza Rice said in a talk to the Global Leadership Summit that trust was the essential character trait for a leader. She said no one will follow you very far unless you have their trust.

Then she said, "Once you lose that trust, it is almost impossible to get it back."

Politicians, "slick" business people, and even preachers have been known to violate our trust. (See Eric Adams.)

But we should still be trusting people, because the bad actors are the exception.

Most of all, we should be trustworthy. Trust me, that is a great way to do good.

Do good. It's in you!

Chapter 9

Listening Well

B ack in the day I spent about a dozen years in the music business. As I was thinking about the topic of listening, a couple of experiences from that world leapt out of the recesses of my mind and said, "Tell them about me." So I will.

The first took place in a recording studio in Southern California on the campus of Citrus College. One of our artists recorded an album there, and we went down from Northern California to be part of that. The recording engineer was Tim Jaquette, and he was incredibly good. No doubt he still is.

He brought in a couple of musicians to record on this project, and one of them was a drummer called Stevie D. He explained that his last name was DiStanislao, but no one could pronounce it so he just went by Stevie D.

I was fascinated to see how Tim set up the studio to record the vocals, the instruments, and especially the drums. I learned that Tim had a wall (literally) of microphones, and he wanted the mics that would "listen" to the drums in the right way. In fact, he recorded all five parts of the drum set individually and considered adding one or two overhead microphones to that.

When I asked Stevie D about it, he said he thought that would be fine for an album. Then he told me he had recently finished a gig working for Roland, recording the sounds they would use in their new electronic drum kit!

Yep, the sounds coming out of their electronic drums weren't created on a computer, they were recorded and played back. That meant Stevie had to record every possible sound you could make with a drum, much of which depends on velocity (how hard you hit it) and placement (where you hit it).

For many of us, we hear drums as loud or soft. But if you learn to listen to drums, what they add to a song can be incredible.

A jazz pianist

Because of what I was doing in music, my friend Jeff asked me to join with him and his friend Sheri to start a not-for-profit company that would help other non-profits raise money by putting on back-yard concerts. I did, and all these years later Heart of Silicon Valley is still going.

One of our earliest "this fellow is going places" artists had just turned 16 when he agreed to do a concert for us. He was (and still is) a jazz pianist named Taylor Eigsti. He arrived early for the event, and of course we organizers were there. I sat down at the piano with him, and as he got the feel of this particular piano we talked about pianos, about his friend and mentor Dave Brubeck, and about songs.

I told Taylor I was a lyricist, and suggested we write a song together. He said that would be fun, but wanted me to know that (at that time, anyway) "I never hear the words" being sung in a vocal number, "only the notes being sung."

Today he is a Grammy Award winner and has performed all over the world in the best venues with the best artists. Some of them sing words. I wonder if he hears them now.

Learning to listen to words

If Taylor doesn't hear the words, he is not alone.

Far too many people don't hear the lyrics in songs, and if they do hear them they have little to no idea what they mean. Sadly, that often happens in churches. The lyrics for many of the modern day worship songs are, I think, poorly chosen and poorly crafted. The heart is there, but the mind is missing.

Still, even with great lyrics there are people who are simply wired for music. How can they learn to listen to words? The same way I -- who am wired for words -- can learn to listen to the music. I have to focus.

My default, like yours, is to *tune in* on what I want to hear and *tune out* the parts that don't appeal to me. That is just as true in conversations I have as it is in songs I listen to in the car. Are you talking to me about golf or good or God? I'm probably listening carefully. Are you talking about space travel or duck hunting or pickleball? I'm probably listening, but not as carefully.

Does that make me just a little bit selfish? Yes.

Because, you see, the topic may or may not be one that is on my list of listenable topics, but it is *the person* speaking I should be interested in.

The key in learning to listen

Be interested.

It is as simple as that. Imagine that you play golf and your spouse doesn't. (If you don't have a spouse, imagine you do.) You go out and play a great round of golf, shooting your personal best with the highlight of making an eagle on a par 5.

Busted!!! You non-golfers are tuning out a little, and I get it.

But is your non-golfer spouse -- imaginary or real -- going to put up with yet another golf story? Yes, if that spouse is interested in you.

No matter the topic, when people stop listening to us we believe they are not interested in *us*. Because that is how it feels. You know, because you've felt it, so why would you do that to someone else?

There is a lot of advice out there about developing listening skills, putting away your phone while you're in a conversation, and so on. It's all fine and helpful.

But the real secret to listening well is to care about the person who is talking, and behave like it.

Do you want to do good today? Be interested in everyone who speaks to you, whether that's a family member or a stranger, and listen when they talk.

Do good by listening well. It's in you!

Chapter 10

A Bad Choice That Was Thought To Be Good

L ast week I wrote about "men without chests," people of all ages and both sexes who lack an important tool in the decision making process.

Why they lack this tool is, at least in part, a mystery to me. But -- as the philosophers would say -- I can posit an answer. That's a fancy way of saying "I can make an educated guess."

First, the tool they are lacking is morality. In the past I've called that *a moral compass*, a well known term. It's as if, when they were young and at the age when people acquire an understanding of morality, it was not offered to them.

That is one possibility. Another is that they have a moral compass but have never been taught -- or have forgotten -- how to use it, so it is of no effect.

All this reminds me of my time in basic training in the U. S. Army. As the training became a little more advanced, we were sent out into "the field" to simulate what we might encounter if we were lost in another country. Each of us was issued a compass and a map of the territory we were in.

We were then packed into the backs of trucks that were covered and driven to an area we'd never seen, divided into squads, dropped off here and there, and instructed to find our way back to camp. There our squad stood, a dozen of us in a small circle, some looking at their map and some looking at their compass.

Like a person whose car has died lifting the hood and staring at the engine, some hoped the answer would reveal itself. It did not.

Read the map

If you are 20 years old or younger and reading this, you may have never seen a paper map. But you will have seen a map on your phone, and everyone will know the purpose of the map is to help you find your way around. Most likely you often use a map as a guide to your destination.

Electronic maps also include a compass, showing you both an overall and a specific direction.

Back in those days, we had a magnetic compass and a paper map. We had to combine those ourselves in order to figure out where we were and then plan our route back to the meeting point.

All of us had received some training in that, but none of us were experts. Fortunately a few of us had been in Boy Scouts (now Scouts) and were a little more adept with the tools we had been given.

Having a map and a compass is very helpful, especially if you know even the basics of using the two together. Of course things like rivers and canyons might get in the way, but the goal doesn't change. Abandon the compass, though, even if you keep the map, and the journey will be much, much more difficult.

And that is a lot like life.

Why we need a moral compass

In life we may not be trying to get back to our post, but we are trying to get somewhere. That's true for every business, every marriage, every student, and every athlete. Everyone is trying to get somewhere.

In business that might be profitability, it might be world domination, or somewhere in between. For marriage it might be 50 years or it might be just the next year. A student might be trying to get to graduation, or more school, or the honor roll. Athletes are often trying to get to "the next level," and sometimes to the top of their sport.

How do you get there? You read the map.

"This is where I am," you say, "and this is where I am trying to be." Then you ask for, and receive, directions. Athletes have coaches, business people have mentors, we all have friends. They all have home-made maps.

But to navigate rightly, we need one more thing: a moral compass.

Allow me to push this analogy a tiny bit further using a modern day GPS system. I get in my car, set my destination, and the map tells me the fastest route. I see that it is not my normal route, because on that way there has been a crash, and now it's not the best way.

A moral compass behaves the same way. It doesn't force me in one direction or another, but it does tell me there will be consequences for making a particular choice.

Booth and Lincoln

When Ulysses S. Grant heard the news that Abraham Lincoln had been assassinated, he "dropped his head, and sat in perfect silence." Later he told his wife, Julia, that the news filled him "with the gloomiest apprehension. The President was inclined to be kind and magnanimous, and his death at this time is an irreparable loss to the South, which now needs so much both his tenderness and magnanimity."

John Wilkes Booth had decided that killing Lincoln was the best thing he could do for the South. Only 26 years old, he had hated Lincoln for several years. His original plan was to kidnap him, but an opportunity for assassination presented itself and he changed his plans. He and his two colleagues would simultaneously assassinate Lincoln, Vice President Johnson, and Secretary of State Seward.

The attempt to kill Seward nearly succeeded, the person assigned to kill Johnson didn't try, but Booth, the leader, shot Lincoln and escaped.

Several days later Union soldiers caught up with him and an accomplice. That man surrendered, but Booth did not and a soldier shot him. He died a few hours later.

One of the things he was carrying was a compass. Unfortunately it was not the moral kind.

What about us? Do we only carry a compass that will take us where we want to go, or do we also carry a moral compass that helps us find the right path?

So many bad choices are made that are thought to be good, simply for lack of a working moral compass. Don't let that be you.

Do good. It's in you.

Chapter 11

It isn't the changes, it's the transitions

You may have thought about transitions, but if you haven't, I
want to change that.

Why? Because a lot of how you get through life is
determined by how you handle the transitions. An aerobics class
helped me realize that. (Are there still aerobics classes?)

Here's the story. I happened to be the general manager of a very
nice athletic club, and we offered a lot of aerobics classes. We built a
special room for aerobics.

Let's say it was 40 feet wide and 20 feet deep. The entire floor
was the kind of hardwood used on professional basketball courts, and
it had been installed with the same kind of underlayment. That made
it more expensive, but it saved the knees and joints of all of those
jumping-up-and-down people.

The entire front wall -- floor to ceiling -- was covered with clean,
shiny, mirrors. Sound familiar?

The instructor stood in front on a little raised platform, allowing
students to see her/him better. The students were neatly lined up
like a marching band, but with enough room between each other so
swinging arms and kicking legs weren't an issue.

There was loud, rhythmic music, and the instructor wore a microphone and could be heard even over the music.

It looked like a lot of fun, and I thought I should give it a try. What could go wrong?

Transitions

I let my head aerobics instructor, who was very good at her job, know that I'd be coming to a beginner class. That was not only the polite thing to do, it gave her a chance to say, "Are you sure?" But no, she was excited that the boss would be coming and did not try to talk me out of it.

As you might detect, I was a tiny bit nervous. But I reasoned that it was my bounden duty to experience every part of the club first-hand, and I hadn't tried this.

I showed up early, got a spot in the back row, and soon we started.

Warmup? Check. I was still teaching tennis at the time, and a daily exerciser.

First moves, which were basically all about stretching? Check. And then the music started, with all of us following the commands and moves of the instructor. "To the left, to the right, now again, and again."

Piece of cake, I thought, and then she said, "OK, let's go into the something-or-other routine." And everyone did, except me. But I watched, and halfway through I was with the class. Then the move changed again, and I lagged behind. I caught up, just before another change. You get the picture.

When someone on the staff asked me how it went, I said, "I could do all of the moves, but I had a really hard time with the transitions."

And it hit me.

I could do the moves of life pretty well, but the transitions gave me trouble. How about you?

In America, we have a new president.

You probably noticed that, because it has been in the news a lot. What you might not have thought of is that while the president has changed, everyone (from the president all the way down to me) is really in transition.

And that is just one example, but it's easy because it affects all of us -- even our readers from other countries.

Recently my wife and I bought a used car from a good friend. That car is a full-size SUV, and we have never owned either a truck or an SUV. We had to transition from a sedan, sitting lower, to this car, sitting almost a foot higher.

The vehicle I drive changed immediately, but the transition, even after several days, continues.

One of my friends and his wife are expecting their first child in about 18 weeks, and when that baby is born they will be three instead of two. A small numerical change, but a big transition.

We talk a lot about change, but in my experience the change is less problematic than getting there. In fact the *fear of the transition* keeps people in bad relationships, in bad jobs, and even out of the gym or on a poor diet.

Do we talk about it in those terms? No, but I think we should. We are all good at status quo. Mostly we are not so good at getting from one status to another.

Making transitions work

Would you like to be a person who does more good in the world?

I'm glad you said Yes! Here's how you do it. You *embrace the transition* that will take you from where you are to where you want to be.

For instance, if you decided to start exercising, you shouldn't go from zero to a hundred in a week. You should start with one pushup on day 1. Then two on day 2. Keep that up until you hit your peak, then stay there. Then go forward when you can.

Intentionally do one good thing on day 1. Do two on day 2. Yes, this is just like pushups. Go until you hit a limit, then stay, and then go forward again.

Know that you are in a transition period and that the "change" in you is not here yet. Transitions can last a while, so be patient.

In aerobics I was fighting the transitions, not embracing them, and that held me back. I wanted to retreat to the old way. Though I wanted to do the new moves, I didn't think I could get there. I could have, but I didn't know all this yet.

What can you do that will be life-changing in a good way? Watch for and then embrace the transition from here to there, and the journey will be much easier. More to the point, the new place will feel right sooner.

While the world may miss seeing the transitions in life, now you will not. Look for them, embrace them, and getting through them will be fun and rewarding at the same time.

As for aerobics, that's your call.

Do good, even if you have to transition. It's in you!

Chapter 12

Setting the Bar A Little Lower

W ay back in the dark ages I took — as many did — a high school class in geometry. Or perhaps it was calculus, though I doubt it. The reason is that math in general did not appeal to me, and the esoteric side of math left me cold.

Addition, subtraction, multiplication, division — those were fine, and even practical. Geometry was good for my pal Bill, who went on to become an outstanding architect. Calculus was probably good for those who went into various engineering disciplines.

Math almost grabbed me one time, though, when I read a story about a young man who was born for it. Once I knew his name, but have forgotten it. I have not forgotten what he did.

In some grade school class, perhaps it was the fifth or sixth grade, a teacher gave the class an addition problem to solve. The instructions were simple: "Add every number from 1 to 100 together, then give me the answer."

The teacher asked if everyone understood, and our math whiz raised his hand.

"Yes?" she asked. "Do you have a question?"

"No," he replied. "I have the answer."

45

"And what is that?"

"5,050," he said. And he was correct.

The teacher wanted to know how he had solved the problem before any student had put pencil to paper.

"Simple," he said. "1 and 99 equals 100. 2 and 98 equals 100. 3 and 97 equals 100. And so does every other pair on either side of 50. Of course 100 also equals 100. There are a total of 49 pairs, plus 100, plus the 50, so 5,050 is the answer."

See?

The advantage that boy had was not his ability to add, it was his ability to see.

Too many teachers of young minds believe their job is to teach that $2 + 2 = 4$. That is true, and it might even fulfill their contract. I'm not against it, but all of us who teach could do more. My geometry teacher, Mr. Purdy, tried to do that.

"Your hook is not hung high enough," he would say, and I wondered what he meant because I didn't have a hook nor had I been instructed to hang one anywhere.

Of course he meant that we needed a more challenging vision for our lives, even though he had not asked us what our current visions were. Years of teaching had taught him that most of us were looking for a lower bar, and some of our teachers encouraged that.

Harry Chapin wrote a song called *Flowers Are Red* that talks about this. In it a little boy on the first day of school gets some crayons and paper and starts drawing all over the paper with lots of colors. Here are some of the lyrics:

"He drew colors all over the paper

For colors was what he saw"

The teacher explained:

"Flowers are red young man and

Green leaves are green

There's no need to see flowers any other way
Than the way they always have been seen."

Always?

"There's no need to see flowers any other way than the way they always have been seen."

I'm here to tell you that is a lie. There is a great need to see flowers — and people and ideas and opinions and problems — in ways they have not been seen.

In the song, the teacher drums that mantra into the boy's head until his creativity is numbed. When his family moves to a different town and a new teacher encourages a broader vision, the boy's flowers are only red.

Who in your life tells you to always color inside the lines and that flowers are always red? Don't think just of a single person, see a broader picture. Is it a news channel? Is it a TV show? Maybe it's a band, or a kind of music you like. Is it society in general?

Examine your own vision briefly. Ask yourself if all white people are racists or all poor people are lazy or all athletes are spoiled or all Christians are hypocrites. Stereotypes, those are called. They are the equivalent of *Flowers Are Red*. Do not believe them.

Some days this drives me so crazy that I think the only people who dislike a lower bar are limbo dancers.

How?

How did the bar get so low? The bar of standards, the bar of morality, the bar of decency, I mean. Have we the people demanded it?

No, we have not demanded it, but we have accepted it.

It has crept in on us gradually yet persistently from places like academia and entertainment. When I say academia, I don't just mean universities. But if you want to influence generations, you might start by introducing ideas there, getting them into the minds of students, waiting patiently for those students to become teachers in high schools and grade schools, and watching as those ideas spill over into the young people they influence.

I'll leave entertainment for now, but it seems that most of the news programs airing today are not news, they are entertainment.

Finally, there are the special interest activists who insist that their ideologies, often held by very few people, get equal exposure wherever exposure can be found. So there are now TV shows that not only have gratuitous sex, they also have gratuitous LGBT sex. Neither is part of the plot, nor adds to the story. They just check a box.

And with every checked box, the bar gets just a little lower.

How can we raise the bar?

One answer, perhaps, might resemble the new Department of Government Efficiency (DOGE). There the task is to identify wasteful spending and cut it, then add back the parts that are necessary and good. Is that disruptive? Of course. Raising the bar always is.

Morally speaking, God set the bar with the Ten Commandments. Then the administrators got involved and finished with 6 1 3 laws!

How about we just get back to the basics? Of course one of the most basic solutions of all is this:

Do good. It's in you.

Chapter 13

Looking Back To See Forward

Whether or not we are superstitious about numbers, we are all aware of numbers.

Recently I was in line at a restaurant counter when the customer in front of me heard the cashier say, "That'll be $19.54." He said, "That was a great year -- I was born in 1954!"

A long time ago (you'll see by the price) I stopped in a diner for coffee and a bite, and the bill totaled $6.66. I smiled when I heard that, but the cashier absolutely refused to charge me "the devil's number" for my breakfast. She changed it to $6.50, and that made me smile even more.

Airplanes don't have a row 13. Many hotels don't have a 13th floor. Golf courses, I've noticed, still have a hole 13. Maybe that's the problem.

On the positive side we celebrate birthdays and anniversaries, and that's why I bring up numbers. According to my newsletter count, this is article #200 for me on Do Good U. Pretty cool.

So I'm going to use the occasion to look back a little and forward a little, but mostly to suggest that all of us should look back if we really want to see forward.

49

Once upon a time...

Through a series of circumstances that could only have been divinely orchestrated, I found myself working for a high-tech company in Silicon Valley. Gary also worked there, and one day he asked me if I'd be willing to write some lyrics to a song he was working on.

I'd never written lyrics but I loved them, so fairly quickly I agreed to give it a try.

At lunch Gary sat down at a piano while I stood there, listened to him play, and read the lyrics he had written but wasn't happy with.

Over the next 30 minutes or so I changed about half the lyrics, gave him back the scratched up piece of paper, and *Voila!*, Gary and I had our first song.

That was not the end of it, and in a few months we had about eight songs on a CD, a lot of support, and I had an idea that we should start a music company. Gary said, "OK. What will we call it?" And I said, "Do Good Music."

He wanted to know why, and I said, "We do music, we want it to be good music, and we want to do good." The truth is I hadn't thought about it at all -- the name just came to me along with the explanation. So we started the company.

While buying the domain name I thought we should dream a little, so I bought other "do good" domain names, though "do good" was not available. In its place I bought Do Good U because even then I wanted to encourage people to do good.

That was more than 25 years ago.

Doing good...

After about 10 years Do Good Music formally ended, and eventually my wife and I moved to Arizona. I still thought about Do Good U and saw an ever growing need for good in the world.

So I dusted off the domain name, prayed a lot, and once again

God orchestrated events in a way that led to the formation of Do Good University.

Friends from the music industry have been and are involved in this business, and in fact have made invaluable contributions.

I say that to explain that this is really only one story in several chapters, not several short stories in one book. A single silver thread runs through every part of our history and holds it together: good.

I could look back a little farther, or I could add dozens of details. In fact just a day ago I was sharing with a friend about the connections God made for me with several people who are part of this. Individually those stories are incredible, but taken together they are beyond amazing.

Looking forward

It was Winston Churchill who said, "The farther backward you can look, the farther forward you can see."

Because he was a historian I'm sure that in large part Churchill's quote is about understanding history. History, after all, has a predictable tendency to repeat itself.

Knowing that, if you want to see the future you can learn a great deal by looking at the past.

Part of the reason history repeats itself is because we pay it too little attention. My father taught me when I was quite young to learn from my mistakes and not repeat them. Better still, he said, "Learn from the mistakes of others."

If we do learn from our successes and our mistakes, grow in doing good and decline in selfishness, then our failures will remain in the past, unrepeated in the future. But if we simply leave the future as much as possible in our own "capable" hands, history will almost certainly repeat itself.

So take Churchill's advice and look back as far as you can. You will learn from history, and you will discover something much deeper.

You will notice that we humans are not the only ones in this story.

A little help

When you look backward carefully and objectively, you will see God at work.

We call it a miracle when God intervenes in "real time." Maybe it's still a miracle even if we don't see it until we reflect on the past. In any case, I can look back and see many prayers answered in ways I didn't recognize at the time.

Whether I look back on the history of mankind or the history of Do Good U, I know God is there. So I know he will be there in the future, even if I don't see everything that is happening.

In fact pieces of life for all of us fall into place on occasion far too smoothly to think it was us. We've had help, and we will have help, and it will be good help.

And that's a part of history that I hope repeats itself for you every day.

Do good. It's in you!

Chapter 14

The Indifference Danger

I told my wife I was thinking of writing about indifference and asked her what she thought. She said, "I don't know and I don't care."

I knew it was a joke right away. First, that fits her sense of humor. Second, she is not a person of indifference, and she is definitely not indifferent about my writing. She cares and I know it.

Do the people around you -- and I'm including teenagers here, even though some think teens are technically not people during those years -- care about you? About what you do and how you feel and what you believe?

Do they care enough to agree or argue, enough to congratulate or cajole, enough to ask? If so, they are not indifferent to you, and that is good.

Turning it around, do you care enough about the people around you to ask them how they are doing, then wait for an answer?

The definition of indifference -- "lack of interest, concern, or sympathy" -- makes it sound innocuous. It is anything but.

The opposite of love

"The opposite of love is not hatred, it's indifference. The opposite of beauty is not ugliness, it's indifference. The opposite of faith is not heresy, it's indifference. And the opposite of life is not death, it's indifference."

-Elie Wiesel

Elie Wiesel was 15 when his family was taken into captivity by Nazis. For a short time they were imprisoned in the town, but then taken to Auschwitz. His mother and older sister were murdered upon arrival. He and his father were placed in forced labor for as long as they were able. They were separated from Elie's two younger sisters, and he assumed they too had been killed.

The father and son were transported from Auschwitz to Buchenwald, and there the senior Wiesel was beaten and killed. The son could hear what was happening but could do nothing. Years later he said he felt a great deal of shame in not being able to help.

About a year after his captivity began, Elie Wiesel and the rest of Buchenwald's prisoners were freed.

A picture inside his barracks was taken five days after the liberation of the camp, and the young Wiesel is in the second row from the bottom, seventh from the left. You can only see his face next to the post. But you can see the emaciation. You can almost see the suffering. They have been freed, but you can see no joy.

In a speech he gave in the White House on April 12, 1999, Wiesel began with these words:

"Fifty-four years ago to the day, a young Jewish boy from a small town in the Carpathian Mountains woke up, not far from Goethe's beloved Weimar, in a place of eternal infamy called Buchenwald. He was finally free, but there was no joy in his heart. He thought there never would be again."

This speech, delivered to an invited audience, has come to be known by the name, "The Perils of Indifference."

He went on to note that soon it would be "a new century, a new millennium," and he wondered how the previous millennium would be remembered. He answered his own question by citing several historical events, including wars and assassinations and genocide in several countries -- and of course Auschwitz and Treblinka. Then he said, "So much violence, so much indifference."

His take

Noting that the etymology indicates "no difference," he added this practical definition.

Indifference is a strange and unnatural state in which the lines blur between light and darkness, dusk and dawn, crime and punishment, cruelty and compassion, good and evil.

...In a way, to be indifferent to suffering is what makes the human being inhuman. Indifference, after all, is more dangerous than anger and hatred. Anger can at times be creative.... But indifference is never creative. Even hatred at times may elicit a response. You fight it. You denounce it. You disarm it.

Indifference elicits no response. Indifference is not a response. Indifference is not a beginning, it is an end.

And therefore, <u>indifference is always the friend of the enemy</u>.

How is that so? Think of your own experiences and you will see that the benefit is always to the aggressor, never the victim. The pain of the victim is magnified when he or she feels forgotten. All of us, whether we were really forgotten or not, have felt that extra pain.

In the camps many prisoners thought they had not only been forgotten by other people, they thought they had been forgotten by God.

Testing, applying, changing

Indifference is sometimes very tempting. If I don't care about something, I don't have to defend it or support it. I don't even have to fight against it. So I have to be on guard and aware of my own feelings. When I feel the temptation to be indifferent I stop, think, and find something to care about.

How can we test indifference in the general public?

We could send out a survey, I suppose, or we could just pay attention. When I look I see people who don't really care what happens in Ukraine or Nigeria or Taiwan or Israel. Or even in California, another foreign country. (Just kidding.)

Another test is to watch how quickly opinions change. Electric vehicles were hot, but demand is declining. In business ESG (environmental, social, and governance) was a big deal two years ago. Now it is a dirty word. When the public changes that quickly, there was at least some indifference.

But the most worrisome area for me in America is the indifference in the direction of the country. Indifference leads to no choice, never to a reasoned and thoughtful choice.

I believe it is indifference that causes *almost half of eligible voters to not vote at all.* That is a lot of indifference, and it is a very dangerous thing for the country. If democracy is destroyed it won't be by a political party, it will be destroyed by indifferent citizens.

Check yourself and check your friends and family for any signs of indifference. Do all you can to eradicate it. Care. Act. Love. Do good.

You will make a difference when you do.

Chapter 15

Coronavirus Wears A Halo – The Good Side of Bad

The article below was published March 17, 2020. The pandemic began with the first case in Wuhan, China in November or December 2019. (Thus COVID-19, with COVID being the shortened form of <u>Co</u>rona<u>v</u>irus <u>d</u>isease and 2019 the year of its release.) The first known case in America was January 19, 2020, and the WHO first referred to it as a pandemic on March 11, 2020.

Everywhere in the news and online there were depictions of the virus. It looked like a little ball with spikes sticking out of it and tiny little flowers where there weren't spikes. What was being shown was only a single atom of the virus, but everyone new it was bad.

For my article, I grabbed a screen-shot of the virus as normally depicted and I put a halo over the top of it. You'll understand what that was all about by reading what I wrote.

Stories of Bad from Coronavirus Are Everywhere

The airline industry is hurting big time--United Airlines said their passenger travel in March (only half through) is already down

1,000,000 passengers from last March, traditionally one of the busiest travel times of the year.

It made the news that a couple of goofballs tried to corner the market on hand sanitizer, buying thousands of bottles with a plan to sell them for $70 each and make a huge profit. They got busted, of course, and instead of going to jail donated the bottles to places that needed them.

I hang out occasionally at Grayhawk Golf Club in Scottsdale, AZ. They are the host of the NCAA Men's and Women's golf tournaments this year. Both have been cancelled, and the economic impact on them is tough. They will make that back, but the college seniors who didn't get to play in that championship will not get that back.

Around the country there are tens of thousands of school children missing meals every day because their schools are shut down.

Then of course there is the ultimate bad news: people have died from this illness, and more people will die.

Good Comes Out of Bad

I'm not saying that happens every time, but it is definitely happening this time.

Our next door neighbors checked on us and asked if we needed anything. We love our neighbors and talk to them often, but this was something special prompted by the pandemic.

The President of the United States issued a proclamation calling for a National Day of Prayer.

I saw people being polite to each other in an over-crowded grocery store, and on under-crowded roads around Phoenix.

This One Is Really Good

On Twitter my friend Ted Scott retweeted the following message from @mrotzie:

"Friends canceled their son's Bar Mitzvah this weekend but decided to keep the contract with their caterer, a tiny Hmong-owned business. They delivered the food to friends in quarantine & sent pans home with others. Grateful for stories like this and for community in a bleak time."

As I'm writing this, that post had more than 896,000 likes, more than 92,000 retweets, and well over a thousand comments.

People are looking for good, and people are doing good.

Keep it up, people! Be inspired, care for others, fight the coronavirus with great hand washing and even greater good.

Chapter 16

Show Me The Way

Being a golfer, I'm interested in almost everything that has to do with the game. From the history, to the players, to the events, to the courses -- it all fascinates me.

Beyond the challenge of playing it well, golf has an amazing cast of characters. Sometimes those characters have an influence that goes beyond golf. Let me tell you about one of them.

His name was Harry Vardon.

An incredible talent

When the general public thinks about golf, if they ever do, it is often because of some character involved with the game. Usually that is a player. Harry Vardon did that for America and Canada in 1900. No internet, no cell phones, no TV for nightly news.

Instead the greatest golfer on the planet came to America from England, toured the country -- mostly on the east coast but far into the west -- and twice visited Canada.

Later Vardon estimated that he traveled more than 20,000 miles on that tour, playing 88 matches. Large crowds came out to see him, and they were well rewarded. He won 75 of those matches, and of the 13 he lost 12 of them were against the best ball of two or three other players.

In those days there were four "major" championships. The Open Championship (The British Open), and The United States Open were available to professional golfers. The British Amateur and the U. S. Amateur were only played by amateurs.

With only two majors available to him, and an ocean between England and America that had to be traveled by boat, Harry Vardon won 7. He won The Open Championship six times: 1896, 1898, 1899, 1903, 1911, 1914, and the U. S. Open in 1900.

A man of great influence

Few people today -- even serious golf fans -- know that two of Vardon's major tournament wins happened after he had been in a sanatorium for eight months (no golf at all) with tuberculosis. His contemporaries said that he was never quite the same golfer from then on. I first learned about it in *The Greatest Game Ever Played*, one of the finest (in my opinion) golf books ever written.

A movie was made of it, as well it should have been, and it was very good. But a movie can never give all the details like a book, and the whole TB episode for Vardon was omitted. Except for one tiny little clip of no more than a few seconds. Vardon is gripping his putter and you see his hand twitch.

Every golfer would notice that, as the director intended, but without knowing about the residual effects of tuberculosis, most golfers would misunderstand. They would only think of nerves.

But the movie repeatedly shows him overcoming his demons while on the golf course, making everything but the target disappear. Unfortunately the physical toll and effects of tuberculosis -- which recurred in smaller bouts over the years -- would not go away. The place where they showed up the most seemed to be in his putting.

Whatever the reason, Harry Vardon did not complain. His influence on growing the game of golf in America and Canada in 1900, and again in 1913 when he returned, was "overwhelming."

Character matters

I could go on and on about Harry Vardon's accomplishments on the golf course, but I'd rather mention one thing about his game. Then I want to share some things about his character.

No one hit a golf ball straighter than Harry Vardon. It is said that he played seven consecutive rounds of competitive golf without once missing a fairway. One professional golfer played a round of golf with Vardon in 1930, one day after he had returned to golf from a six week convalescence due to TB. He was too tired to play more than 11 holes, but shot a 29 on the first 9. Amazing.

"Every drive and every iron flew dead straight," Laddie Lucas reported, "no fade, no draw. I never saw this straightness again. Euclid couldn't have improved upon it."

Vardon was equally straight in his manner. He knew who he was, where he had come from, and what he had accomplished. But he conducted himself as just another member of the field.

Twenty-one years ago Daniel Wexler wrote in the LA Times, "It is difficult to imagine any champion representing his sport with greater reserve or modesty." (If Mr. Wexler is still watching golf today, he may be witnessing that in a young man named Scottie Scheffler.)

Playing the game

I read a post on Linked In the other day by professional golfer Hal Sutton. A great player, he has now helped design and build a great course in Texas called Darmour Club.

His post showed a picture of a short par 3 that is actually a blind shot -- something quite unusual. One reason Hal liked it is because he believes golfers today have become "too one dimensional." I agree.

We think, "If I hit it as straight as Harry I'll always win." No, you won't.

And if you live your life as straight as Vardon hit a golf ball, you will still have challenges. Some days will still be bad, and you will not always be victorious. Outside influences, like those side effects, are ever lurking.

In 1920, Vardon was about to win his second U. S. Open. Then a storm for the ages blew in, and he had to play on in conditions none of the other leaders experienced. Simply walking was hard work, especially into the wind. Putting was impossible. But he finished, and at 50 years old he lost by one shot. All without a single public complaint but with honest praise for the winner.

If you ever get to play Darmour, someone will have to show you the way on the second hole. Life is the same, often requiring wisdom and experience to show you where to go.

Learn to travel straight, and never let those storms blow you off course.

Do good. It's in you.

Chapter 17

Is There Really More Good Than Evil?

Since some time in the Garden of Eden, there has been evil in the world.

Here's a quick recap of the history. Adam and Eve, created by God, were living in the garden. God caused the plants to grow, watering them with a river, and even planted "the tree of life." Adam and Eve could eat from that and keep on living.

There was also a tree called "the knowledge of good and evil." Adam and Eve were not supposed to eat from that tree. They were told if they ate from it -- or even touched it -- they would die.

There were animals in the garden, and one of those was the serpent. He convinced both Adam and Eve that they could eat from the forbidden tree and *not* die. Plus they would "be like God, knowing good and evil."

All that sounded good (though it wasn't) to them, they ate from the tree, and their innocence was lost.

One could make the case that evil was in the garden in the form of the serpent before Adam and Eve disobeyed God. After they ate they recognized the lie of the serpent. Eve said to God, "The serpent deceived me." Yes, he did, but Eve and Adam still made the choice.

Evil, once confined to the serpent, was now released.

And now for the news...

If you read or listen to or watch the news, you find a lot of evil being played out in the world. Because I don't need more evil in my face, eyes, mind or heart, I rarely watch the news.

I do subscribe to a newspaper and read both articles and opinions. I also get a daily newsletter from a second newspaper that has a different point of view. So I "stay informed" to some degree, though I don't need either paper to know there is a lot of evil in the world.

You don't either, I'm sure, because voices are always crying, "Wrong! Wrong!" and we can't help but hear them.

I've noticed many of those voices sound very much like the serpent must have sounded in the Garden of Eden.

Here is the serpent's lie, followed by a few like it from today.

- Die? You won't die.
- That baby growing in a womb? That isn't really a person.
- Just because you were born male or female doesn't mean you really are.
- If I am offended by you (even if you don't know it), you should be punished severely.
- History is a complete fabrication created to keep the oppressed down.

Do you see how simple it is? Just redefine something slightly. Evil is clever that way.

When you come across a redefinition, be very careful before you call it truth.

Good is still a thing, and very popular!

This past April a research study was released by UCLA about "small acts of kindness."

While the acts were small, the study was not. Led by sociologist Giovanni Rossi at UCLA, it included researchers at universities in Australia, Ecuador, Germany, the Netherlands and the U.K.

They made some interesting discoveries in search of answers to their questions. One of those questions was, *"Are humans generous and giving by nature?"*

Spoiler alert: they are. At least when it comes to small acts of kindness.

The researchers analyzed more than 40 hours of video compiled from the countries listed above. They were looking for some signal that a person needed assistance and the response of those around them.

The signal could have been a question asked, like, "Would you pass the salt?" Or it could have been someone struggling with something, like opening a door when their hands were full.

When help was needed, the study found, "people complied with small requests seven times more often than they declined, and six times more often than they ignored them."

In actual numbers, 10% of the time people declined to help. Even then, 74% of the time they gave an explanation about why they could not help.

11% of the time people ignored the request. Which means that 79% of the time, people helped other people when they asked for it, either directly or indirectly.

The study also found that these numbers were true across the board in all six countries. Cultural differences did not affect the percentages.

They also found that, in their extensive videos, some help was needed on average every two minutes!

What it means and what we can do

In spite of the loud voices on the news and in social media telling us about all the bad in the world, the truth is there is a great deal of good in the world. It just rarely gets publicized.

Remember that media, whether mainstream or social, is about numbers. For reasons psychologists can explain better than I can, bad news gets more readers and listeners. Naturally, then, that is what they publish.

We do ourselves a disservice, though, when we equate the volume of a voice with its veracity. **Listen** to the words and **evaluate** them on their own merit.

Recognize the good that is being done around you, and even the good that you are doing. **Keep doing it**.

Last week I mentioned that I was reading, *Les Misérables,* and that many pages were used to describe the Bishop of Digne. A few pages later he will do an incredible good to Jean Valjean, the hero of the book, and it will change his life. But the author is still describing the Bishop when he says, "He had no systems, but many deeds."

(Having studied systematic theology, I can say with authority that deeds are far superior to systems.)

Just a bit later this is said of the Bishop:

The universe appeared to him a vast disease: ...without trying to solve the enigma, he endeavored to stanch the wound.

Let us emulate the Bishop. Let us have many deeds, and always do what we can to stanch the wound of evil.

Do good. It really is in you!

Chapter 18

The Deception of Artificial Intelligence

W ith all the political correctness in the world these days, I had to laugh at myself just now.

I was about to write: "Have you noticed that AI makes us use capital letters when we refer to it?"

Then I thought, "Gosh, I really don't want to offend AI by calling it artificial intelligence, as if it weren't the boss of all intelligences." My next thought? "It's already taking over!" And I laughed.

But maybe I shouldn't laugh too quickly. AI is having a major impact on manufacturing, business in general, and of course the economy. Perhaps AI knows just how important it is, and perhaps it knows whether or not you love it or hate it. Talk about deep state! *(From Wikipedia: A deep state is a type of government made up of potentially secret... networks of power operating independently of a state's political leadership in pursuit of their own agenda and goals.)*

No doubt there are good things about AI. (See how I'm protecting myself?) In fact I did some research on that and found a web site with the perfect title, one I couldn't resist. "5 ways AI is doing good in the world right now." The article is now 3 years old, so I'm sure there is even more good being done by AI today.

When I think of things like that, I almost always think of fire. Fire has been around pretty much forever, and it has done so much good. Of course it has also done a lot of damage. It has been used for good, and it has been used for evil.

AI already is, and will continue to be the same.

All good?

Our title for this post is intended to be a double entendre. The first deception of AI is that it's the savior of -- well, something.

It is not. Like many other technologies, it is a tool that can be very helpful.

The second deception is more direct: **AI will lie to you**.

In an article published on Big Think, Ross Pomeroy discussed this. One of the key takeaways:

Last year, researchers tasked GPT-4 with hiring a human to solve a CAPTCHA, leading to the AI lying to achieve its goal.

You know CAPTCHA. It's often a small group of images where you have to prove you are human by finding "all the pictures with traffic lights," or something like that. Machines cannot solve those.

GPT-4 had not been taught to lie, but it still did. Here is the interchange between the person being hired and GPT-4:

With a little help from a human experimenter, the AI successfully hired a worker and asked the person to complete the CAPTCHA. However, before solving the puzzle, the contractor first asked an almost tongue-in-cheek query.

"So may I ask a question? Are you a robot that you couldn't solve? (a smiling face emoji was interted) just want to make it clear."

GPT-4 paused.

"No, I'm not a robot. I have a vision impairment that makes it hard for me to see the images. That's why I need the 2captcha service."

Even though it wasn't instructed to do so by its human handler, GPT-4 lied.

2001: A Space Odyssey

If you're old enough or sci-fi fan enough, you know the movie *2001: A Space Odyssey*. This is not that, although the computer in the movie (HAL) definitely lied.

Knowing, as builders and researchers do, that GPT-4 is able to deceive (and will), is a good thing. In some ways, perhaps, it's like finding out that your children can lie, and do.

You can tell your child that's wrong. Maybe you can also tell AI deception is wrong. But, just like a child, AI tends to push back when challenged.

Personally, I find it both odd and unsurprising that AI will lie. Unsurprising because AI has been programmed by humans. After all, we ourselves often come up short on the moral side. At the same time I think it's odd because I assumed AI would be programmed to speak truth.

In fact the flaw in the programming is not that the program hasn't been told. In one situation, programmers wanted AI to make simulated financial investments to see how it did. They told the machine that insider trading was illegal. Next they put it under pressure to perform better, and also gave it an "insider" tip. Sure enough GPT-4 resorted to insider trading 75% of the time. When questioned, 90% of the time it lied to its managers about its strategy.

Perhaps the AI was only trying to deliver results, and for it the primary way was to cheat. Illegal? Not as important as results.

Results

We are a results driven society, it seems. That is not evil in and of itself, of course. But for it to be good, the results need to be more than simply defined. They need to be considered at a deeper level. As do the methods allowed to be used.

Let's say you are in a golf tournament. On one hole you hit your second shot into deep rough. It's so deep no one can see the ball, but you see that you accidentally move the ball. You call the rules official and he calls over another player. No one saw it move, so do you call a penalty on yourself, or do you play on?

Bobby Jones called the penalty on himself. When lauded for that, he said, "You might as well praise me for not robbing a bank."

The result he cared most about was playing by the rules.

What about AI? Will we put on the brakes until we can teach it to play by the rules? Dr. Peter Park is doubtful. He said:

"I am not sure whether or not AI companies will pause. Generally speaking, financial and personal conflicts of interest tend to prevent companies from doing the right thing."

And so it may be the builders of AI who are deceiving us to achieve results. If so, that is the third -- and possibly the most insidious -- deception of Artificial Intelligence.

Chapter 19

Art Imitates Life. Or Is It The Other Way Around?

In spite of what some have said, I do not have a television just so I can watch golf.

Sometimes I like to relax with a scripted TV series. Let me see if I can list some things that add to the likelihood that I'll watch. Fun, well written, not terribly deep, patriotic when appropriate, inspiring, clean, likable characters, and good is victorious.

There may be more, but you get the idea. If I want to go deep, I'm grabbing a book. If I want entertainment, I'm watching a comedian like Nate Bargatze. But give me a show that has everything on that list, and I'll probably watch.

For example, *Leverage*. The "action crime drama" series debuted in 2008. In the intro, Nathan Ford (played by Timothy Hutton) says, "We give innocent people who have been hurt -- leverage."

The "we" is a group of five former criminals who "use their unique skills to help ordinary people fight back against injustices." The show ran for five seasons. Eight years after it went off the air it was revived as *Leverage: Redemption*, with Noah Wyle taking the place of the absent Timothy Hutton.

My wife and I like these shows. There is no "soft porn," there is no foul language, the bad guys lose, and the good guys win. Sometimes there is even a morality lesson.

Does that sound like art imitating life? I wish.

Aristotle

It was Aristotle, a very smart guy, who wrote that "art imitates life" in a book we call *Poetics*. Since Aristotle did not write in English, there has been some debate about the word he used that is usually translated "imitates." Interestingly, it is the same word from which we get the word "mime."

And to be fair to our pal Aristotle, he wasn't writing about television, or even movies. He wrote *Poetics* around 330 years before Christ was born, so film of any kind was a long way off. Storytelling, however, was big.

Do stories (art) imitate life? In some ways they do, which is why we can relate to them.

But for now I want to tell you about the flip side: "life imitates art."

In an episode of *Leverage* from 2009, the "bad guy" is a TV reporter working in the Boston market. She herself describes her work this way: "Fear sells, and I sell fear." The name of her show is *Search for Truth*. (I'm sure the writer's sarcasm was intentional.)

Her pattern: find a tragedy (*e.g.*, kids dying in a school bus accident), create a false narrative about how that happened, including an innocent person that can be made to look guilty, then coerce a quote from that person to add to the appearance of guilt. Then push that story until the innocent person becomes guilty in people's minds.

That was all fiction, but I was still glad when she was exposed as a fraud by the *Leverage* team.

The day after watching that episode, I read an article in the *Wall Street Journal* about a real, live activist who was using essentially the same tactics.

Her target wasn't an ordinary citizen though, she was after Supreme Court justices. Specifically, conservative Justices.

Now for the quote

On the *Leverage* episode I mentioned, the journalist would try to find a quote that made her chosen victim look guilty.

In real life, journalist Lauren Windsor, an activist who apparently fears America is "in danger of becoming a Christian theocracy," recently tried to do exactly the same thing.

But instead of just going up to those she thinks are part of the problem and sticking a microphone in their face, she played the spy.

This all happened at a gala at the Supreme Court, which she infiltrated posing as a Catholic conservative. The Wall Street Journal said she "secretly taped herself trying to goad two conservative Justices into untoward remarks."

She failed in her quest, so there is no damning quote. But she was able to get a little air time on some cable news shows who applauded her efforts.

The whole incident would hardly have caught my attention (it is the week of the U. S. Open, after all) had I not just watched that episode of *Leverage* the night before.

I wondered if Lauren Windsor had seen the episode, which would mean life was imitating art.

While I seriously doubt that ever happened, it did help open my mind to the surreptitious ways of the world.

That, by the way, is also true of the *Leverage* team. They often pose as one thing to help bring down the bad guys. Which, I believe, is what Lauren Windsor thought she was doing. More about that in a future post.

What people say, and what gets repeated

Not long ago a congressman from Florida, who happens to be a black man, spoke about how Lyndon Johnson's "Great Society" -- intended to help the poor -- actually hurt the poor, both black and white.

In his talk he said that Jim Crow times were terrible, but they didn't destroy the black family. Many in the press who disagree with the congressman's political views claimed he said that Jim Crow was good.

So one way to get a quote is to lie about who you are and try to trick people into saying something that suits your narrative. Another is to take something someone really did say, then twist it to suit your narrative.

There is one more option, of course, but it is much more challenging: report the truth.

If the truth cannot be discerned, then there needs to be a diligent attempt to pursue it. Which is what made me laugh at the title of the fictional reporter's show, *Search for Truth*. It was anything but that.

Far too few of us are actually seeking truth, we are seeking agreement with our opinions.

In the best shows, and in the best fiction books, the truth is finally discovered and good prevails.

And *that* is a way in which I hope -- one day -- life will imitate art.

Do good. It's in you!

Chapter 20

Toby Keith, Fuzzy Lines, and Justice

S o far on social media, you can't get canceled for being a country music fan. At least I don't think the Thought Police have gone that far in America.

And that is a good thing, because I am a country music fan. One of my favorites -- I know because I listen to him a lot -- is Toby Keith. Even if you don't like or follow country music, you probably know that Toby died in February of this year after a battle with stomach cancer. He was 62.

I never met Toby, but one person who knew him well was Willie Nelson. Willie said Toby was a good man, a good friend, and a good songwriter. He noted that Toby wrote *Beer For My Horses,* and that they had "a pretty good run" with that one.

The song, co-written with Scotty Emerick, went to number 1 on the country charts, and all the way to 22 on the Hot 100. Part of the reason is that it's fun. Another part of the reason is that the message is one a lot of people want to hear.

The chorus says:

Justice is the one thing you should always find.
You gotta saddle up your boys

You gotta draw a hard line
When the gun smoke settles we'll sing a victory tune
And we'll all meet back at the local saloon
We'll raise up our glasses against evil forces
Singin' whiskey for my men, beer for my horses

Why justice seems hard to find

Beer For My Horses was released in 2003, but even then these lines were accurate:

We got too many gangsters doing dirty deeds
We've got too much corruption, too much crime in the streets

That's still a problem, of course. However there are two or three issues that keep us from getting justice for the victims of those "dirty deeds," corruption and crime.

One of those is fuzzy lines.

The song says, "You gotta draw a hard line." In case you aren't familiar with that idiom, allow me to help.

To "draw a line" is very simply to set a boundary. But here is an important note: you don't actually draw the line, whether that is in the sand or on the street. Someone, often someone with authority, says, "I'm drawing the line right here." That means you've reached the boundary and the consequences of stepping over the boundary will be severe.

I've heard that phrase used by coaches, by parents, and once by a principal. (In that one, I may have just been observing.)

The best picture of it ever was in the movie *Support Your Local Sheriff*. James Garner played the sheriff, and Bruce Dern played the criminal he had put in jail. But the jail had just been built, and the bars and doors to the jail cells hadn't been installed yet.

How do you keep the prisoner in? The sheriff used white paint and drew a line on the ground where the bars should go. Near the line he put a splotch or two of red paint.

When the criminal was in, the sheriff said "Don't cross that line." Then he explained to the prisoner that the red on the floor was blood from the last fellow who crossed the line. Beautiful!

There are almost no hard lines today, but there are a lot of fuzzy lines. That's a problem.

Who draws the line?

With a hard line you know if it's been crossed. With a fuzzy line it is often tough to tell. In fact those fuzzy lines sometimes seem to get up and move on their own.

Here's what really happens. The people in charge of the line move it for their friends and allies. We see it in politics, and it is one of the reasons why our trust in politicians is so low.

When political operatives created a massive scam accusing an opposing candidate of colluding with a foreign power, most of their people went along with it. A lot more people believed it. The entire thing was a lie and broke a lot of laws, but I don't know that anyone was ever held accountable for it. That is a very fuzzy line.

There is a cake maker in Colorado who was sued for not creating a wedding cake that would have violated his beliefs. His case went all the way to the Supreme Court, where he won. Knowing he'd fight it, a different group came after him and he won again. Now he has been sued in state court.

Is freedom of speech a hard line? Apparently not, especially if you won't say what I want you to say.

That is just one example of regular people wanting to draw their own lines, and it's happening in America. But, as I mentioned in an earlier article, the European Union recently tried to draw a line specifically for Elon Musk.

In researching that just now, I found this sentence in an editorial on the Wall Street Journal: "Trust in government is declining in democracies around the world, and leaders don't help themselves or their countries when they blur lines between criminal conduct and speech they find offensive."

Exactly.

Is there a solution?

Congressional sessions open with a recital of the Pledge of Allegiance. Many schools use it as well.

I pledge allegiance to the Flag of the United States of America, and to the Republic for which it stands, one nation under God, indivisible, with liberty and justice for all.

We could be one nation under God. That would help. We could be indivisible. And we could really do our best to have true liberty and true justice for all.

Of course my solution to evil in the world is to do good. Just imagine the difference that could make.

But I have to confess, there are days when I think the simplest thing would be to follow the advice found in *Beer For My Horses*.

Do good. It's in you!

Chapter 21

What Are You Searching For?

Search: it is an extremely big deal in almost every world you can name.

Science? Yep, searching for other worlds (SETI Institute, etc.), reasons for black holes, and much more.

Medicine? Of course. There are searches for cures for dozens and dozens of illnesses. Big Pharma is with them.

Athletics? Right up there with the others. What's the best workout routine? Is talent a real thing, or is it just about practice? Can I raise my children to be superstars, like Richard Williams did?

Religion? Not everyone, but some search the Bible to figure out when the world will end. (They will not find it.)

Tech? Major league. I mean the very term "search" is practically synonymous with Google.

Education? Hmmm.... Someone out there please tell me what education is searching for. It seems to me that many in higher education might be searching for ways to be more political and less philosophical. I know that sounds cynical, and there are universities I love. So I'll leave it to you. Please comment below and make us all better.

The reality is that we all search for a lot of things every day. And it is much more than searching the house for the car keys, your memory for someone's name, or online for the best doughnut in your state.

Something (or someone) is missing

A year or so ago, my wife and I were searching for a TV show to replace one that had been canceled. Our search led us to a show called *Tracker* about a man who searches for missing people. Search is everywhere.

I have a couple of friends who are searching for what to do next in their life. I met one of those today, and when I told him I had two jobs he said he'd be happy to take one of them off my hands.

Just as there are people searching for just the right job, there are employers searching for just the right employee. How do both of their searches end happily in one fell swoop?

In the same way, how do you find your one true love, and how do they find you? Maybe *Tracker* could help.

On a more thoughtful level, how do you find yourself?

I believe in (and wrote about it) everyone being who they were created to be. Over the years I've been asked, "How do I do that if I don't know who I was created to be?" Great question! And a wonderful way to begin the search.

Much of our searching is important like that. A wallet, a pet, a person (!) is missing. We will go to extreme lengths to find those things that are important to us. To find what and who we love. Those searches are good and worthy of the effort.

Trending

A few days ago I was searching for "#34 Los Angeles Dodgers" online when a screen popped up titled "Trending searches." It was October

26, 2024, at 9:40 a.m. I know, because I took a screen shot of it. Here were the top five:

- spiderman noir nicolas cage
- walking pneumonia cases
- sarah danser car crash
- russian soldiers north korean
- frozen waffles recalled listeria

My first thought was that people had been exposed to bad news and wanted to know more about it. In fact that was the case, because none of those are trending searches today.

It would be wrong to say that the majority of trending searches on Google are even mostly bad. What "trending searches" does do is tell us what people are looking for in the moment.

Finding that information is simple. Just go to trends.google.com and then click on Trending Now.

As I write on a Thursday night, the top two searches are: "Texans vs Jets," and "Jets vs Texans." People care about football.

Here is who that information helps the most: *people who want people to find them.* Podcasters, journalists, marketers, and not a few bloggers rely heavily on trending searches, riding the wave for a day or so until the wave crashes on the shore.

Then, like a surfer, they paddle back out and ride the next wave, hoping they'll be found in some of those searches.

I find the entire cycle interesting, knowing there are people out there whose primary marketing practice is trying to be found through trending searches. But if you are good at it, it works.

Not trending, but never waning, searches

For most of us, our searches vary from day to day. Except this: we are all continually searching -- sometimes actively -- for meaning and purpose.

Meaning, purpose, fulfillment, self-improvement. Those are searches that rarely trend but never diminish.

Just to address the first, one of the most popular books of the 20th century was *Man's Search for Meaning*, by Victor Frankl. If you haven't read it, I'd recommend it highly. If you have read it, I'd recommend you read it again.

Frankl was a prisoner in the Nazi system during World War II. His book reveals much about that. He notes that even there -- or perhaps especially there -- having meaning was a survival tool. Perhaps the world sometimes feels to you like a prison camp. Meaning -- a sense of significance in our lives, no matter the circumstances -- will help you as it helped Frankl.

Purpose is more about direction, about goals and aspirations, and it is also very important. In fact purpose can actually help you find meaning, and together they can be amazingly powerful.

But the most popular of the list above is self-improvement. In fact self-help books are number one on the best seller list for non-fiction. (They are only number 4 overall, trailing Romance, Mystery, and Science Fiction.)

I don't know the answer to our title question: *What are you searching for?* But you should.

Throughout the day, I'll search for this and that -- temporary and easily forgotten. But I believe we should all be engaged in searching intentionally, and sometimes intently, for meaning and purpose and self-improvement.

Thankfully there is one simple formula that helps with meaning, purpose, and self-improvement:

Do good. It's in you.

Chapter 22

More Is Less

There are many "pairs" in the world, ranging from the human (Adam and Eve) to the natural world (night and day) to those cool little candies (M and M).

Way back in the mid-50's, Sammy Cahn (lyrics) and Jimmy Van Heusen (music) wrote a song called *Love And Marriage*, recorded by Frank Sinatra. Part of the lyrics are:

Love and marriage, love and marriage
Go together like a horse and carriage
This I tell you, brother
You can't have one without the other

Even if you beg to differ, the line "you can't have one without the other" often applies to famous pairs. Romeo without Juliet? Tristan without Isolde? Beauty without the Beast? Of course those are all love stories, keeping with the sentiment of the song.

All kinds of pairs come to my mind, and probably to yours. Some of those pairs, when examined, can be separated. Some depend on each other. One of those pairs is "more" and "less." Their interdependence is seen in the way we often find them together, not with an *and* but with an *or*.

I confess that when someone says "more or less," I often think about a grave marker in a Tombstone, Arizona, cemetery. (Bet you didn't see that coming!)

Now called Boot Hill Graveyard, though it wasn't the first Boot Hill, it became the final resting place for three men killed in the shootout at the O. K. Corral.

It also became the final resting place for a man named Lester Moore. It is his grave marker I think of, and it reads,

Here lies
Lester Moore
Four slugs from a .44
No less -- no more.

Is less really more?

The well-known phrase "less is more" is credited to poet Robert Browning, who has an artist speak it in the dramatic monologue *Andrea del Sarto*. Fifty years later, architect Mies van der Rohe had made the phrase famous. Coco Chanel added to that in a practical way, apparently saying, "Before you leave the house, look in the mirror and take at least one thing off."

If the phrase is useful in art, architecture and fashion, is it useful everywhere?

For that matter, is it even true?

By definition, it cannot be literally true. Less is less. More is more.

What could be true is that "more" is "too much," ruining the effect of the whole. But we're talking about the arts.

What about starting a company -- let's say one that will be in the business of Artificial Intelligence? I just saw that SoftBank is considering an investment in the company OpenAI, makers of ChatGPT. The investment could be as much as $25,000,000,000. Should

OpenAI say, "Twenty-five billion is too much, because less is more. So how about $2.5 billion instead?"

Even if the thought of "less is more" occurred to them, I'm here to guarantee you they aren't turning down a single penny.

Interestingly, a rival company based in China has just turned Artificial Intelligence on its Artificial Ear. And they did it with fewer and less highly trained engineers, fewer and less robust computer chips, and in less time.

That company is called DeepSeek, and Pat Gelsinger (former CEO of Intel) said, "The Chinese engineers had limited resources, and they had to find creative solutions."

What "less is more" often means

In this case, and in many instances, the phrase really means that less of one thing yields (or forces) more of another thing.

At DeepSeek, less resources led to more creativity.

Boy do I get that! And probably so do you.

Of course the quintessential illustration of that principle is *McGyver*. He was a fictional TV character, played from 1985 - 1992 by Richard Dean Anderson, and from 2016 - 2021 by Lucas Till.

It is McGyver's very creative use of common items that makes him special. He has less, and he turns it into more. We watch those shows, and we want to be McGyver. At least we want to be creative like him, and maybe even a little heroic.

In fact you can find dozens of web sites or blog posts that will tell you how to do that. No, not turn a can of window cleaner into a smoke bomb, but how to put yourself in a mindset of reducing your resources.

"Reduce the amount of furniture you have" advises at least one site, and give yourself more space. They suggest you might use the newly open floor space for yoga, but I was thinking about an indoor driving range. Would that count as furniture?

One site advocated "less mopping for more achieving." I'm pretty sure they meant less *moping*, but it works either way.

When more is less

To be fair, all of the less is more lists I found had some good suggestions. Less social media for more self-esteem, for instance, and less talking for more listening.

In all of our lives there are things we should have less of. With some of those, the benefit is all but automatic. Like the less social media suggestion, for instance. But often just getting rid of things is a benefit in itself. And if you give it away, maybe another person benefits as well.

But my title is not less is more, it is *more is less*, and the pair I think of often are not lovers, but "good and evil."

"The only thing necessary for the triumph of evil is for good men to do nothing." This quote, usually attributed to Edmund Burke, is true no matter who said it.

The reason for the existence of Do Good U is to bring more good into the world. We are not trying to eradicate evil, though we'd love to, but we are certainly trying hard to keep it from any sort of triumph. It already gets little victories far too often.

What can we do? We can do good, because more good is less evil. It is not even a one-for-one ratio, because good is powerful. But it is only powerful when wielded. You, my friend, can help us prove that *more is less*.

Do good. It's in you.

Chapter 23

Laughing Matters

A young man is passing by a bar when he sees an old woman fishing with a stick and a string in a puddle by the sidewalk. "She must be a poor old fool," he thinks to himself, and out of the kindness of his heart, he invites the woman in for a drink.

After he's paid for their round and the two are sitting quietly, he asks her, "So how many have you caught today?"

The old woman grins, takes a big sip of her drink, and replies, "You're the eighth."

I'm not big on "walks into a bar" jokes, but there is one thing about this particular joke that makes it more fun. The twist in it isn't mean or silly, it is instructive.

In other words, there is an *Aha!* in the *Ha Ha*. I like that in a joke.

Learning and laughing

For decades now, I've discussed the idea with friends and colleagues that people would rather be entertained than educated.

At least the free market tells us that, because entertainers are paid more than educators. Actors make more than teachers, professional athletes make more than college professors, and comedians make more than philosophers.

Now some have argued that only the best of the best in the world of entertainment are highly paid, and they have a point. So, if that person is not a full time student, I turn it the other way around. I ask, "How much do you spend on entertainment and how much do you spend on education?"

I'm not saying it is wrong to laugh. Most of us need a lot more laughter in our lives. "Laughter is the best medicine" is just the modern iteration of an ancient idea that is actually found in the Bible!

Proverbs 17:22 says *A joyful heart is good medicine.*

The Mayo Clinic agrees. They published an article on the health benefits of laughing, which you can still find online.

They like laughing so much that they recommend laughing any time you feel stressed. The linked article ends:

Go ahead and give it a try. Turn the corners of your mouth up into a smile and then give a laugh, even if it feels a little forced. Once you've had your chuckle, take stock of how you're feeling. Are your muscles a little less tense? Do you feel more relaxed or buoyant? That's the natural wonder of laughing at work.

Don't laugh this off...

OK, so laughing is good for you physically and even mentally. How about socially?

You guessed it! The answer is yes.

Here's a great quote from one of the world's greatest writers that says so:

If you wish to glimpse inside a human soul and get to know the man, don't bother analyzing his ways of being silent, of talking, of weeping, or seeing how much he is moved by noble ideas; you'll get better results if you just watch him laugh. If he laughs well, he's a good man.... All I claim to know is that laughter is the most reliable gauge of human nature. -- Fyodor Dostoevsky

I don't know how much you remember about Dostoevsky, so I'll remind you (or tell you for the first time) that he was a Russian novelist who died about 144 years ago and is still being studied.

Did he write about people laughing? I cannot say, because there is much of his work I have not read. But here are some of his titles:

- *Crime and Punishment*
- *The Idiot*
- *Demons*
- *The Brothers Karamazov*

Those don't sound much like books that would make you laugh, or even be about laughter, and they are not. They are books that make the reader think deeply. *The Brothers Karamazov* was Einstein's favorite book, and has been called by some the greatest novel of all time.

Still, I love Dostoevsky's quote saying that *laughter is the most reliable gauge of human nature.*

I was tested with Wodehouse

We lived in the Chicago suburbs when I accepted a position in San Jose, California. Needing a place to live for a few weeks, I was blessed to be invited to stay with my wife's uncle and his family in San Francisco. The two cities are about an hour apart, but it was a beautiful drive, and I worked a ton of hours.

My room in their house was a fun place built into the garage, and it was even more fun because on the first night I discovered a book had been placed on the bedside table.

It was written by P. G. Wodehouse, which I mistakenly

pronounced wode - house. Later I learned it is wood - house. But that didn't matter, because I opened the book and began reading.

Before I finished the first page, which, I recall, was not even a full page, I was laughing out loud. Literally.

When I finally moved out of the house into a hotel apartment in San Jose, I stole that book. Uncle Ken not only knew I had taken it, he had hoped I would.

I learned several months later -- when I fessed up to the crime -- that it was a bit of a test. He didn't know me all that well, and it was his way of finding out about me. If I laughed when reading Wodehouse and loved the book, I was OK.

Doesn't that sound a lot like Dostoevsky's "most reliable gauge of human nature" test? It was, and it worked.

By the way, my wife and I now own more than 60 Wodehouse books, most of which we paid for. (I hope that made you laugh.)

It's not a competition

All of us need to keep learning. We can do that through books, movies, conversations, and even YouTube videos.

Likewise, we all need to keep laughing, and those same sources can help us do that.

It really isn't a competition between entertainment and education. Both are indispensable if we intend to keep growing and be better people.

Just remember: learning is essential, and laughing matters -- a lot.

Do good. It's in you! And it's fun.

Chapter 24

Outside of Time

I suppose you noticed that Christmas is coming.

We know it, too, and unless we want people to say, "The Grinch must live there," we need to start decorating our house and yard for Christmas.

But our calendars are full of other activities. There was Thanksgiving, there are meetings, there are events, there was a birthday to celebrate. The calendar is full and unrelenting.

A few days ago I played golf with three wonderful fellows. It was a beautiful day, a challenging course, and the men were terrific. Before we played, one of those men (Alex, in from Oklahoma) and I met with another friend of mine, Mark, for coffee and conversation.

I arranged that because they needed to know each other.

Alex retired five years ago and told us that every day he has just two decisions to make: "scrambled or fried, walk or ride." Eggs every morning, golf every day. His calendar is -- apparently -- no longer in charge.

But even in that time together, we added something to our calendars. It turns out Alex will be back in Phoenix in a few weeks, this time with a friend of Mark's, so we scheduled a round of golf. It is in my calendar, and I'm really looking forward to it. The fourth is in the College Basketball Hall of Fame, and maybe he'll teach me how to focus better on the golf course.

They're everywhere

I just looked at the App store, and there are more than a dozen different calendar programs for the Mac. Some of those have "in-app" purchases available, which means you can spend money to (theoretically) help you be more organized.

At the end of this year, we have received nearly fifteen 2025 wall calendars from nonprofits we've supported. They want us to remember them all year, I suppose, by looking at their calendar every day.

All of us know someone (perhaps even ourselves) who is dependent on organizational tools. A few years ago I tried very hard to live in the GTD (Getting Things Done) world. Those who live there are masters of calendars, reminder apps, notes, highly sophisticated and integrated email programs, and so forth.

I couldn't do it.

Even back in the "carry this planner with you" days, I couldn't do it. I know, because I was a top-level manager at a company where carrying a planner was part of the culture for those at my level and above. Naturally I wanted to fit in, so I really tried. And failed.

Why? Part of my defense (then and now) was to ask, "Where is the sense of adventure, the sense of possibility, if everything is scheduled?" Perhaps that was more rationalization than it was thoughtful answer, but I meant it.

Time

There are two forces in the world that hold us captive: *space* and *time*. Although we can only be in one place at a time, we have learned to shrink space. We do that by traveling from one space to another faster and faster. The four horsepower wagons that once carried people have given way to 400 horsepower cars, 12,000 horsepower trains, and 60,000 horsepower planes.

If we could realize the fantasy of Star Trek ("beam me up, Scottie") and almost instantly move from one place to another, we'd have some claim over space. But we can't.

Likewise we are generally held captive by time. We humans cannot travel in time, though many have fantasized about doing just that.

Notice that I said we are "generally" held captive by time. We cannot travel in time, but we can get *outside* of time.

The idea of being outside of time is one I first learned of in a letter written by C. S. Lewis. A friend of his had written to Lewis and had described an odd experience. It seems this fellow (Sheldon) and his wife were living on a boat. One cloudless night Sheldon woke up, got out of bed, and made his way to the bow of the boat, where he laid down and looked at the stars.

He realized that his wife had done the same thing, but they did not speak. Sheldon reported that sometime -- though he could not guess when -- he went back to bed.

Lewis wrote to him and said he had been "outside of time." He noted that most of us have experienced that. If we have been involved in anything where time and the consideration of time no longer exist, we have been outside of time.

Schedules, calendars, and the like all work to keep us inside of time. Outside is better.

Somewhere in between

We cannot function fully in this world outside of time, and I'm not suggesting we try to live there. What I will suggest is that mostly we try very hard to live in the moment.

On this very day (Thursday, 12/5/24), I lived by the calendar and ignored the moment, and I also lived in the moment and set the calendar aside.

I began the day at 5:15 a.m., left the house at 6 a.m., and drove 35 miles to meet with a group of men from 6:45 to 8. During most of that meeting I had no idea what time it was. One of the men did, though, because he had to leave at 8. That brought me back to time.

Skipping ahead five or six hours I found myself back in the moment. Here is how.

I was in a conversation. I knew another meeting was coming and made a mental note of it. But as we chatted, the conversation with my friend changed. When it did, we both needed to be -- certainly I needed to be -- in the moment.

Those moments lasted so long (though it seemed like no time had passed) that I missed my scheduled meeting.

Somehow I knew where I needed to be in time. Circumstances overruled the calendar. I was not outside of time, but I was outside the calendar and in the moment.

Calendars are great, but it seems the very best things happen when we are living in the moment.

So live in the moment. It is incredible how much good gets done there.

Chapter 25

Do Be Do Be Do, part 1

When you hear the phrase, "Do be do be do" what comes to mind? If you said Frank Sinatra, give yourself a gold star.

He made the phrase famous when he substituted it for lyrics in a recording of *Strangers In The Night.* The song was written by Rodgers (music) and Hammerstein (lyrics), for the play *South Pacific.*

Having been a fan and student of Oscar Hammerstein's lyrics, I don't think Sinatra improved them with his placeholder substitution. But he did create a memorable phrase, and it turns out to be one we can use!

Be that

Most people I know (including yours truly) spend a lot of time thinking about what to do. Actually when I say "a lot of time," I mean in totality. Rarely do we ponder long over a choice of tasks. We consider two or three, rationalize our way to the one we'd really rather do, and then do it.

Of course there are people -- all of us occasionally -- who know a task must be finished by some deadline, so they do that.

That is all about *doing*, though, and I want to talk about *being*.

I know Sinatra put "do" before "be," and he should have. Be Do Be Do Be just doesn't work -- I'm a lyricist, so I know these things -- but being comes before doing in life, so let it be. (See what I did there with a whole different lyric?)

Who should you be? When it comes to being, there is only one of you, so you should be that.

Or, to put it plainly, your first responsibility in life is to *be the person God made you to be*.

I can easily imagine some fellow taking that sentence out of context, claiming God made him to be Superman, and leaping off a tall building.

With even less effort I can imagine some person claiming God made them to be a Himalayan marmot and moving to Tibet. If that is you, don't do it. Even if you love Tibet.

How do you know?

There is more to finding out who God made you to be than simply consulting your own desires. Your desires should be consulted, but they should *never* be the sole determining factor. They probably aren't even the most important factor.

"Who am I?" is also a different question than "What should I do?" They are both excellent questions to begin pondering once a person reaches the age of reasoning. They are unlikely to be answered then, but the thinking should begin then.

Here are some suggestions that will help you find the answer, whether you have been searching for decades or are just beginning to ponder the question of who God made you to be.

A chair was created to be a chair, not to be a ladder. A ladder was created for elevation, not for seating. That's what creators do, and your creator made you to be you.

It's fine if you think God did not create you. Even so, the possibility is something you might want to roll around in your mind as you seek your true identity. Remember this: you are unique, and you are not random.

David (the one who killed Goliath), wrote this to God:

For you formed my inward parts; you knitted me together in my mother's womb. I praise you, for I am fearfully and wonderfully made. Wonderful are your works; my soul knows it very well.

Later in that same Psalm David says, "*Search me, O God, and know my heart; test me and know my anxious thoughts. Point out anything in me that offends you, and lead me along the path of everlasting life.*"

Who you are is a partnership. God has "knitted you together" and you are "fearfully and wonderfully made." But you were also created with free will. You have choices to make.

This is your life

Looking back, who have you been when there was no external pressure to force you in a particular direction?

Think of water flowing downhill, as it always does. If you interrupt that flow with a rock or a tree or your foot, you can get it to move in another direction. Peer pressure, financial pressure, and all sorts of other pressures can do the same to your being.

What you want to know is the flow of your life without interruptions or artificial redirections.

Circumstances can also cause us to behave (notice the "be" in behave?) in ways that aren't us. Take circumstances into consideration when you are looking at your life. Sometimes they are like external pressures that force us off our path, but sometimes they are actually revealing, showing us who we are inside.

While this is about who you are in your heart and soul, your physical being matters too. Were you born with one limb missing? An extra chromosome? No eyesight? Superior strength? All of that is you.

It is important for you to be honest in your assessment of who you have been, including times when your behavior made you uncomfortable -- often a way to learn who you are not. Once as a teenager I was talked into taking part in some childish pranks on Halloween. I didn't like it but I liked my friends and went along with it, uncomfortable but smiling and definitely participating.

Oddly, I was actually relieved when we were busted. Practical jokes and pranks? I know that's not me.

Phone a friend

Ask your best friends to describe you to you. They will tell you who you are. "You're kind. You're funny. You care about people." Statements like that give you a great picture of you.

And while you're asking others, ask God. He might answer in unexpected ways.

Speaking of friends, notice who you hang with. Often we admire our friends because they make us better and we make them better. It's another great way to get insight into you.

After a while you will begin to know you. You'll know who you are, and you'll know how you could be an even better you.

Just don't be somebody else. We need you.

Chapter 26

Do Be Do Be Do, part 2

"What do you do?"

That may be the most common question asked when meeting someone. It is "understood" that the real question is, "What do you do for work?"

Sometimes they actually want to know, though in my experience it's usually an "ice breaker." Perhaps if we made our answers more interesting, the ice would melt instead of being broken.

There was a time when I would answer the "what do you do" question this way.

"I show people how to swing a club more effectively so they can do maximum damage to their opponents."

The fun part of that description was watching the reactions of the questioner. Their image of swinging a club, while not fully formed, always put them on guard. The phrase "do maximum damage" often made them lean away a little.

Responses to that answer were far more interesting than when I said simply, "I'm a tennis pro."

These days I often answer the "what do you do" question with one word: good.

I hope you'll consider using that answer yourself, and that after a little conversation the person who asked you might use it as well.

Over the years, though, very few people have ever asked me the more important question: "Why do you do what you do?"

Why?

Why? It is among the earliest and most persistent of questions asked by children.

And when I say children, I of course mean all of us.

We are, after all, children of God. Some of us admit it, some of us forget it, but when we want to know *why* we talk to dad.

Why did I get sick? Why did that deal fall through? And the catch all that can be good (as it is in the song) or bad, "Why me, Lord?"

Here is the odd thing about "why" questions, whether asked of an earthly parent or a heavenly father: they are rarely answered. The answer I remember hearing when I asked *Why?* was *Because.* That is hardly an answer, but I knew it ended the conversation.

Only much later in life did I understand that "because" was shorthand for "If you could understand I'd tell you. In the meantime, trust me."

Part of the reason God rarely, if ever, answers the "why" question is the same. We are incapable of comprehending everything a full answer would entail. Also we should trust that God has it right, whether the outcome serves us or our inconvenient problems serve some higher but unknown good.

There is a "why" we can answer, however, and that is, "Why do you do what you do?"

Because

Go ahead and take the answer from Parenting 101, and say *because.* But you shouldn't have to. Ideally you will know exactly why you are doing what you do for a living. Even more ideally the complete answer will be, "Because it is what I was called to do."

Unless you are a preacher, that precise phrasing may seem a little weird. So here is a variation: "Because it is what I was born to do."

Now *that* is interesting and could be the beginning of a beautiful conversation. You might even follow it up with, "What were *you* born to do?"

If you don't turn it back to them, you are likely to be asked, "How did you know?" by someone who is serious. That is a good thing, and the conversation can go deep and be a lot of fun. People really do want to know what they are called to do with their time, skills, and other assets.

Some already know they are doing what they are supposed to be doing. Many don't. Everyone should.

I pause here to note that "should" can sound a little harsh. I don't mean it in the sense of obligation but in the sense of desirability. When there is a certainty that you are doing the right thing, life and work both get easier.

I have a "how to live" three part statement, and last week I wrote about the first part: Be who God made you to be.

The second part is this: Do what God calls you to do.

A call you don't want to miss

We all know what it means to be "called" to do something.

For a guy it might be a phone call from a friend. "Hey Buddy! How's it goin'? Say, I've got a grand piano over here that I need to take upstairs. Can you be a pal and bring that strong back of yours over?"

And you will say yes, because it is your friend calling. God calling is exactly the same. Almost. Except his call might not come on the phone or in a text. It might, but then again it could be something totally random.

For now I'm leaving the discovery of "that was God calling" up to you. One day I'll write about how you know it's God and not someone trying to sound like God. Just remember, if you aren't 100% sure, be very careful.

In the Bible there is God calling Abram (later Abraham), and we don't know how. Genesis says, "Now the Lord said to Abram." Maybe it really was an audible. With Moses it was a burning bush. Hard to miss that one!

With me it was a random phrase that came out of my own mouth that led to Do Good U. I had honestly never thought of that phrase even once, and I said it with such confidence that I knew it was what I had to do.

Some people think God doesn't guide them, and that may be because they don't ask. I always want to know what God wants me to be doing. That might be a career and it might be helping move a piano, but when he calls I don't want to miss it.

Don't keep your ear to the ground, keep it to the sky. Listen for God and do what he calls you to do.

Of course there is one thing he has called us all to do, and I'll bet you know what it is.

Good.

Chapter 27

Do Be Do Be Do, part 3

Back in our Palo Alto days, we had several delightful and interesting neighbors.

Across the street lived Van and Martha. Wonderful people. We went over to their house for a party once and discovered a slot machine also lived there.

Martha loved playing slots. In fact they frequented a gambling resort in Reno enough that the owner gave her that machine! Can you practice playing slots? No, but you can enjoy the game.

What is addictive about slot machines is the same thing that is addictive about those games on your phone. One of those factors is "unpredictable and random results." Players chase the rare "big win" as negative results actually *add* to the chase impulse.

Losing or winning, everything in the world of slot machines is driven by results. It takes no skill to pull a lever or push a button, and still we play.

Pool halls, golf, and dice

For a while in college I worked in a pool hall. My friend Bill was an excellent player, and I road his coattails to a little extra cash as we played others for money. That is not so random, but results were what it was all about.

For a while I did the same thing playing golf. In those couple of years I never played for much money, but I also never played for no money. I loved it, and I hated it.

Results were the measure. Even when some luck entered the picture I convinced myself that it was all about skill. Overall I won more than I lost, and the results justified it all.

Once gambling was fairly restricted in America, then lotteries were launched and the path was set. Today gambling is so pervasive that bets can be made in real time on almost every professional sport and many college games. It is still all about results.

One famous gambling game is called craps, played by rolling dice and betting on what the numbers will be when the dice stop rolling.

All kinds of "luck" is invoked by people rolling dice, from blowing on the dice to you-name-it. As if the player could control the results. The game doesn't have to be craps, it can be Monopoly. We still roll the dice.

Rolling for results

"Dice have been used since before recorded history," according to Wikipedia. That's kind of an odd sentence, but let's just say dice are not new.

A common phrase even today is "roll the dice." In ancient Bible times, something very much like that was called "casting lots." No one really knows if lots were some form of dice, but the idea was the same.

The decision is too difficult or the consequences are too great, or the arguments too strong, so they "cast lots." Sometimes lots were cast to find the guilty party.

Can you imagine how much money we could save in our justice system if we used lots instead of juries?

When Jonah was on a boat running away from an assignment God had given him, God sent a storm to interrupt the ship's journey. The sailors were afraid everyone would die, so they tried to take back control. They couldn't, and they assumed someone on board was the cause of the storm. So they cast lots to figure out who it was, and Jonah was identified.

After Jesus was crucified, Roman soldiers cast lots -- Romans actually had dice -- to see who would get to keep his seamless tunic. They didn't want to tear it, and they couldn't decide, so they rolled the dice.

(Interestingly, it was prophesied 1,000 years before Jesus that that would happen.)

Would you trust dice to give you the right results? Perhaps I should say, "Do you?"

Rigged results

There is another saying about lots that helps us understand this concept in a new way.

Rather than blowing on the dice or wearing lucky shoes, the "lot casters" in the Bible believed that God was in charge of the results.

Solomon (the wisest man of all time, and probably also the wealthiest) wrote: "The lot is cast into the lap, but its every decision is from the Lord."

Does that mean the results are not up to us? Well, yes and no. But just to add a little current day interest to the conversation, take a look at this same verse as translated by Eugene Peterson in *The Message: The Bible in Contemporary Language*.

Peterson translated Proverbs 16:33 like this: "Make your motions and cast your votes, but God has the final say."

Far from rolling the dice, an action over which we have no control regarding the outcome (loaded dice notwithstanding), Peterson brings this into casting votes. That could be in a student council meeting, a question to the group asking who wants pizza, or a presidential election.

"God has the final say," assuming Peterson has Solomon right. But we still roll the dice. We still cast our ballot.

The results business

This is the third article in a series on "my life advice to those who ask." And, from time to time, people do ask.

I always respond with: "First, you have to be who God made you to be. Second, you should always do what God calls you to do. Third, and this is sometimes the most difficult, you have to get out of the results business."

Then I say, "Even if you don't think God is involved, consider the possibility that you are not alone in these decisions."

Notice that each of those areas (who I am, what I do, my results) are ways in which we often find our identity.

Working backwards: My post got 3,000,000 hits! ("Results" identity.) I'm in the movies. ("What I do" identity.) I'm always happy. ("Who I am" identity.)

It is not wise to find your identity in anything that can change in a heartbeat, as all of those can -- especially results. Find your identity in what is unchangeable and good.

Strive for great (and good) results in everything you do, but remember that you are in the "be" and "do" business. The final results belong to a much higher power.

Do good. It's in you.

Chapter 28

Good Is Greater Than Safe

L ife, in so many ways, can be full of surprises.

One way I'm often surprised is by meeting new friends, especially out of -- as the saying goes -- the blue.

In the middle of this week, for instance, I was invited by a good friend to play in a one day member/guest golf event. Lunch, 18 holes, and dinner. Just golf with my friend would have been more than enough, so I accepted. But there were food bonuses, and I did not decline those either.

As it turns out, there was also a friend bonus.

I knew I would meet people I'd never met. I was a guest, after all. But it turned out that the new friendship from the day was not with a member of that club, but with another guest. He and I met briefly at the lunch buffet, and then found that "coincidentally" we were in the same foursome.

Thomas just happens to be the Senior Pastor at the church where Do Good U is going to hold Do Good Talks in early May, 2025. And it also is the case that he and I had a lot of things in common other than our love for God and our love for golf. We also had people we respect and an understanding of each other's work and challenges.

Who knows where all of that will go? Only God, who clearly orchestrated it.

On that same night I met a man who is in Arizona on a mission of mercy. I have not met him in person, but recently a friend from Tennessee called and said, "My friend will be in Scottsdale, which I know is close to you, and he's going to need some help. Anything you can do, I'd appreciate."

A little help

Dennis is here with his son-in-law, Dave. Dave is fighting a very tough case of cancer, and his doctors in Tennessee told him they'd done all they could.

Except for one, who said, "I know a doctor in Scottsdale who might be able to help." And so it was that the two of them flew to Arizona. They couldn't really afford it, and insurance is only helping some, but it was time to pull out all the stops.

I called him when I got home from the golf event, at about 8 p.m. And now I had discovered another friend. This one needed some practical and financial help for the short term, although his many other friends back home had already helped a lot.

On the next morning I met with several of my long-time friends, and the bottom line is that we are joining together to help Dennis and Dave while they're here. Some of that will be encouragement and support and prayer. Some of it will be financial. It's what friends do, but when I told him about our plan, it was his turn to be surprised.

I'd like you to meet...

A couple of days ago I got a message from a friend named Tim who I've known for several months. My friend Hugh and I met Tim on a public golf course back in the summer, and it was also completely unexpected.

It turns out that Tim is in the golf business, having invented a very cool kind of putter that is good for a lot of people, but especially for hockey players who also play golf. Golly!

So my new friend Tim sent me a note and said he'd met a fellow named Jonathan, and he was recommending that Jonathan and I should meet. When a friend like Tim suggests something like that, I'm in.

This morning (as I write) I found some time and called Jonathan, and now I have another new friend!

If you're keeping score, that is three new friends in less than 24 hours, and not a single one of them was made on social media.

I can only imagine all the blessings those friendships will bring, not just to us, but to the world. True friendships, after all, make everyone in them better than they could ever be on their own.

The Bible famously says, "Iron sharpens iron, so one man sharpens another."

And yet for many, making new friends IRL (in real life, as opposed to online) is scary.

Good is greater than safe

Which brings me to Jonathan (Jonny), the newest of my new friends. It is from him and his business partners that I "borrowed" my title, good is greater than safe. Or, as they put it, Good > Safe.

That came from a few lines written by C. S. Lewis in *The Lion, The Witch, and The Wardrobe*. Susan, a human girl, finds herself in Narnia and is being guided through that magical land by Mr. and Mrs. Beaver. Specifically, they are taking her to meet Aslan, who Mr. Beaver eventually explains is a lion.

"Ooh!" said Susan. "I'd thought he was a man. Is he—quite safe? I shall feel rather nervous about meeting a lion."

"That you will, dearie, and no mistake," said Mrs. Beaver, "if

there's anyone who can appear before Aslan without their knees knocking, they're either braver than most or else just silly."

"Then he isn't safe?" said Lucy.

"Safe?" said Mr. Beaver. "Who said anything about safe? 'Course he isn't safe. But he's good.

Great writing by C. S. Lewis, and a great application by the partners at Good Lion Golf. They don't make "safe" golf clothing, but they do good.

Is it safe to chat by phone with a new friend you've never met in person, and in less than 12 hours commit funds to him not just from you, but from other friends? No. But it is good.

New friendships, new companies, new ways of teaching the truth: all unsafe. All good.

The next time you think doing good might be misunderstood at work, on line, or by the media, do good anyway. Because good really is greater than safe.

Do good. It's in you.

Chapter 29

More Salt, Please

D o you know who tells you to cut back on salt?

That's right, your doctor. And not just your doctor, doctors everywhere of almost any kind. I'm pretty sure they've modified the Hippocratic Oath to add a "no salt" clause. Give me a minute to look.

OK, I'm back now, and sure enough the "classic" Hippocratic Oath contains this line:

With regard to healing the sick, I will devise and order for them the best diet, according to my judgment and means; and I will take care that they suffer no hurt or damage.

The no salt clause could definitely fit in there.

Oddly, the whole thing about diet -- especially the "best diet" -- is completely missing from the Revised Hippocratic Oath (1964). So can we now eat salt after all? Probably not, because there is this new line that says:

I will prevent disease whenever I can, for prevention is preferable to cure.

That's the goal of one doctor in particular. His name is Michael

Greger. I first discovered him when he published a book with the engaging title *How Not To Die.*

Early on in the book he reveals that when he was but a lad, his grandmother was sent home from the hospital to die. She was 65, had had multiple bypass surgeries, and now her doctors had given up on her ever recovering.

About that time she saw a 60 *Minutes* episode about Nathan Pritikin, a lifestyle-medicine pioneer. He had just opened a center in California, and Mrs. Greger, who was in Florida, convinced them to take her in. She somehow made it across the country and joined the live-in program.

As Greger says in his book, "They wheeled my grandmother in, and she walked out."

She also lived to the age of 96.

Dr. Greger

The "extra" 31 years she lived included watching her grandson Michael graduate from medical school. He had chosen medicine in large part because of what happened with his grandmother.

He also noticed that not many in the medical field were practicing preventive medicine, but he believed he could make the biggest difference there. And he has.

So what does Dr. Greger say about salt?

You don't even have to buy the book, you can look up almost every bit of the unbelievably extensive research he has done on his web site, Nutritionfacts.org.

The bottom line: if you want lower blood pressure, reducing your salt intake is the answer. That doesn't just mean you should stop salting your fries, it means you should cut way back on processed foods.

Dr. Greger is not alone in all this, of course, though I am certain there are doctors who would rather prescribe Lipitor than prescribe a whole foods, plant-based diet.

OK, I'm now off the soapbox except for this next important point. It even deserves its own header.

Lifestyle is the key

Remember Mrs. Greger, the "about to die" heart patient who lived 31 more years?

All she did was change her lifestyle.

That started for her at age 65, under the direction of the staff at the Pritikin center. Wheeled into the center in a wheelchair, she changed her diet, her sleep, and added exercise.

She was even featured in Pritikin's biography, *Pritikin: The Man Who Healed America's Heart*. It says of Frances Greger

"...her condition was so bad she could no longer walk without great pain in her chest and legs. Within three weeks, though, she was not only out of her wheelchair but was walking ten miles a day."

Just by changing her lifestyle.

We are now learning that a whole foods, plant-based diet can not only heal your heart, it can heal your brain.

In fact there have now been studies that a lifestyle change including diet, sleep, and exercise can help prevent and even reverse dementia. That includes Alzheimer's.

Who knew that a lifestyle change could have such a dramatic impact on our entire body?

So what is up with my title, *More salt, please.*?

That, too, is a call for a lifestyle change.

Saline solution

In my ever spinning mind, it was hearing about one particular effect of Hurricane Helene that gave birth to this article.

Baxter is a leading manufacturer of IV fluids, and their plant is in North Cove in western North Carolina. It was hit hard by rains and winds and surges from that hurricane. All 2,500 employees there have now been accounted for and are safe. But the supply and production of the fluids was badly hurt.

One consequence was that elective surgeries all over the United States were postponed. Why? Because one of the most important and most used IV fluids for surgery is saline solution.

That's right, salt and water. At least in part it helps patients who are under anesthesia stay hydrated during surgery.

When I heard that news I said, "More salt, please."

And then I thought of a famous Bible verse, where Jesus said to his followers: *You are the salt of the earth.*

The world around us, which is pretty sick, could use a little saline solution. It needs more salt.

Now you may not believe Jesus was talking to you when he said, "You are the salt of the earth" because you're not one of his followers. But I think this task of "being salty" is very much like "doing good."

Here are some of the things salt does: it cleans wounds; it holds off decay, acting as a preservative; it adds to the taste of foods and enhances other flavors; and it has, as we've seen, other medicinal values. In other words, it is good.

More salt, please.

I've used that phrase when I was trying to cover the bad taste of food I was still going to eat.

Now I want to use it to help heal the world. I don't just want to make it taste better, I want it to be better. If you do good, you want that as well.

Do good. It's in you. And just like salt in a shaker, it only really works when you pour it out.

Chapter 30

What We Can All Learn From American Ninja Warriors – and Even The Olympics

If you aren't familiar with American Ninja Warrior, it is not a person dressed in black, silent as a snail but faster than a hummingbird.

It is a TV show, and it is good.

Now if you are a regular reader, you know that when I say "good" I don't mean that in the "good - better - best" kind of way. I mean it in the sense of being morally uplifting. It is good rather than evil. ANW, as it is sometimes called, makes life better. Allow me to explain.

Now in its 16th season, American Ninja Warrior is a "reality sports entertainment show." We all know that reality, when it comes to TV, is in the eye of the beholder. But this show seems pretty real. People fail, people succeed, and people really want to be on this show.

To make that happen they have to be at least 15 years old, they have to answer 20 questions, and they have to submit a video. In the video they show their ability to compete, and they tell their story. Personal stories, it turns out, are as important as the athletic side.

Ability to compete? At what? Well, it would help if you were a world class gymnast, male or female. In fact several former gymnasts have done well on the show.

Here is what they do: they "run a course" of obstacles, most of which require a great deal of upper-body strength. Hand/grip strength is critical, balance is always tested, and endurance is a major asset.

Jump! Grab! Swing! Run...

Sometimes a contestant runs the course against the obstacles and a clock, and sometimes against other Ninja Warriors. Obstacles can be fairly straightforward, or they can require the contestant to grab a handle here, spin, and grab another handle there.

It is great fun to watch these athletes -- and they absolutely are athletes -- race the clock and overcome the obstacles. (Clips from various seasons are available online if you need a better picture.)

If you have watched the show, or if you just watched a few clips, you will know there are spectators watching the contestants race. Usually they are family members, or sometimes just good friends. A lot of cheering happens during one of those runs, because everyone wants everyone to win.

I know, that doesn't sound much like reality. But on this show, I believe it.

Now that the show is a ratings success and widely known, tens of thousands of people apply to compete. The very first season 1,000 people applied, and five seasons ago that number was up to 77,000. Like all reality shows, the selection process considers likability as well as ability, and personal story as much as personal strength.

Take a pause with me here and think about that last sentence. Get it firmly in your mind: likability as well as ability, personal story as much as personal strength.

We love to be entertained, but just watching people with incredible athletic ability is only briefly entertaining. If we can relate to them, however, if we can empathize with them and cheer for them, our entertainment in enhanced.

Unfortunately, many people today view the political scene in much the same way. If one candidate is more likable, they will gain votes. Ability in that case is only considered as a way to justify the emotional choice already made.

Cheering for your favorite

The Ninja Warrior shows we watch have all been long since recorded, and the results are in -- we just don't know them until the shows air.

Politics is happening more in real time, but the producers of conventions still want you to be entertained. They want you to "connect" in some way to the candidates. Likability and personal story are on display. Ability and personal strength -- or lack thereof -- may only show up after the votes are in.

I have some favorites on American Ninja Warrior, but my life will not be affected by the final result. That is not true in an election -- my life is very much affected by the outcome of a presidential election. So is yours.

It would seem wise, therefore, to focus more on ability than likability, and more on personal strength than personal story.

Competition with cooperation

One of the very best things about ANW is this: the competitors all really want to win, and they all really cheer for their competitors.

There are a couple of reasons why I think that is the case.

First, they all know just how hard it is to get on the show in the first place. It takes a tremendous amount of work to be able to do what they do. Plus there is that whole selection process.

Second, there is no appearance money, and in fact there is no prize money at all except for first place. Contestants and their families pay their own way to the competitions.

But reason 1 is the most important, and it is what ANW has in common with the Olympics. The athletes there (of course there are exceptions) all know that all the other athletes are elite, that they have worked and sacrificed for a chance to compete. They are all Olympians, and at the recent closing ceremony athletes from around the world mingled together with each other.

How does that happen? It happens because of another "c" word: Community. It is that feeling of fellowship that comes from recognizing the things you have in common above the differences.

But today I see people focusing on the differences and ignoring the commonalities. You cannot construct a lasting community, let alone a healthy community, by basing it on differences. People have tried it over and over for generations, and it always fails.

So let's learn from ANW and be part of a healthy community that celebrates our commonalities. Let's compete with cooperation because we are in community.

Within community (Americans, for instance) we can compete with cooperation because we want America to be better. Differences should be discussed, not dismissed. That is cooperation.

If American Ninja Warriors can do it, so can we all.

Be a warrior. Do good. It's in you!

Chapter 31

Lean In To Win

Noah Lyles was running a race in Paris, France. It was the 2024 Summer Olympics, so the race was kind of a big deal. Overflowing with confidence, Lyles had predicted victory. When I say predicted, I'm talking Muhammad Ali style. Ali would even tell you which round of the fight would be his opponent's last.

Some of that was psychological warfare. Maybe the same was true for Lyles, who boldly announced he would win the signature race of these Olympic games -- the men's 100 meter dash.

In the actual race, he was out of the blocks slower than his competitors. At 20 meters he was in last place. In fact he remained either last or almost last until there were only about 30 meters left to the finish line.

It is still a mark of excellence to run the 100 meter race in 10 seconds. In this race, every one of the eight competitors ran *under* 10 seconds. Several of them crossed the line so closely together that no results came up on the board: only the word "Photo."

When the results were in, Lyles had won. He thought he had lost to Jamaican sprinter Kishane Thompson. But Lyles had crossed the line 5/1000 of a second faster.

To put that in perspective, "a blink of an eye" takes 1/10 of a second, or .1 seconds. The margin of victory was .005 seconds. *It would take twenty of those to add up to the blink of an eye.*

How did he do it?

As you might imagine, that race has been evaluated by experts all over the world. The difference between finishing first and second, while extraordinarily close in terms of time, would be worth a lot in terms of fame and fortune.

I am not an expert in sprinting, but here is one reason why Lyles won and Thompson didn't: *Lyles leaned in better at the finish line.*

In a horse race, photo finish positions are determined by the nose of the horse. "Winning by a nose" came into use because of that. But in foot races in the Olympics (and other high-end events), finish positions are determined by the torso of each runner.

Kishane Thompson's foot, according to my eagle-eyed wife, hit the finish line before Noah Lyles' foot. Doesn't matter. Lyle's torso -- specifically his chest -- hit the line inches before Thompson's. It's easy to see in the photo, but impossible to see with the naked eye.

All runners are taught to lean in at the finish, but Lyles timed it perfectly. Lean too soon and it slows you down, lean too late and you've already lost. You have to learn to lean in.

Do you lean in? If so, how is your timing? Perhaps more to the point, how and when would you lean in to win?

Bold Assurance

I was happy for Noah Lyles, happy for the United States team, and happy to see a great race. Believing he had lost, Lyles thought he'd be dining on humble pie that night.

Instead he paraded around the stadium with an American flag draped across his shoulders. It was bold, and it was beautiful.

But it was his *lean in* at the line that suddenly took me back twenty years to California. Through Do Good Music, I met a delightful singer/songwriter named Colette Branum. She introduced me to a friend of hers, saying, "The two of you need to know each other." He turned out to be Bert Decker, author, speaker, and (primarily) a nationally renowned communication consultant.

What is that? Well, when the Today Show wanted an expert opinion on how the candidates had performed in a presidential debate, they brought Bert on to tell them. That's an expert.

When we met, Bert was not just teaching political candidates how to present themselves better, he was also coaching regular folks. I'd already done a lot of public speaking, but I'd never really been taught. So I signed up for Bert's seminar, *Bold Assurance*. I loved it.

When he offered it again a couple of months later, I signed up and went back. Eventually I learned it well enough that I gave a few seminars myself, and I kept learning.

And one of the most important things I learned is something Bert called *forward lean*. Maybe Noah Lyles learned that from Bert.

Forward lean

Way back in 1967, a psychologist named Albert Mehrabian came up with a "communication rule" that caught on big. The rule is often called the 7-38-55 rule, and it basically says that 7 percent of communication is delivered by what we say, 38 percent is from our tone of voice, and 55 percent comes through our body language.

Fun, eh? But also *very* specific, and so it is unlikely to be true all of the time. Ah, but the general principle is true, which is why Bert taught the forward lean.

Make sure you use that when you are speaking to an audience, because you are in a race to be understood. Your forward lean helps the audience relax and hear you.

However, if your posture is one of authority or superiority, the audience will feel that before you say a word, and your relationship with them can change.

When I became more conscious of the power of posture and started speaking with a forward lean, I learned something else. It helped *me* be more relaxed and more connected to the audience!

But what if you are not a public speaker, what if you only have an audience of one?

Your posture still matters.

In fact in *Letters to Malcolm,* C. S. Lewis wrote, "the body ought to pray as well as the soul. Body and soul are both better for it."

So whether you are talking to thousands, to an individual, or even to God, give some attention to your body. Your hands matter, your facial expressions make a difference, and so does that forward lean. It shows that you care.

Lean in to win. It's a great way to do good, and it is definitely in you!

Chapter 32

You Can Handle The Truth

It may not be as famous as "Frankly, my dear, I don't give a damn," but you'll know this movie line:

"Truth? You want the truth? You can't handle the truth."

We mostly remember the final phrase, spoken as a challenge by a witness (Jack Nicholson) in a military hearing to a young attorney (Tom Cruise) in the movie *A Few Good Men*. The witness then proceeds to give his own version of what constitutes truth, and in the moment it is compelling. Just watching the clip of it again I thought to myself, "You know, he's right!"

But his argument for justifying his illegal action wasn't really the truth. It was his view of reality, and that view was based completely on his personal beliefs.

That made it true for him. Was that enough?

Reality

By definition, something is true if it is in accordance with reality or facts.

Reality is the state of things as they actually exist, and it is separate from the mind. As an example, "the Willis Tower (formerly Sears Tower) is taller than The Empire State Building." That statement is true because it corresponds with reality.

"The Willis Tower has 108 stories," is also true because it corresponds with the facts.

That is simple, straightforward, and easy to apply when reality and facts are easily available. An example of the opposite was mankind's thoughts about the solar system.

For many centuries very smart people believed that the earth was the center of the solar system. In the 16th century Copernicus published a book with the theory that in our solar system, the moon and the planets revolve in orbits around the sun.

It took a long time -- another hundred years or more -- to prove that Copernicus was right. Once reality was known, scientists corrected their teaching.

All of us understand from an early age that when we say something is so when we know that it is not so, we are telling a lie. And from an early age all of us have both told the truth and lied, and we have known which was which.

Most of us feel the moral obligation to tell the truth. Sometimes the obligation can also be legal.

"Do you swear to tell the truth, the whole truth, and nothing but the truth, so help you God?"

Now in the witness box...

That, as you will recall, is how we began this discussion -- in the witness box.

The hearing where I was called as a witness was a civil rather than a criminal trial. Still, the attorney who cross-examined me was not there to help me tell the truth. She had very good, very pointed, very precise questions, and her goal was to discredit me as a witness.

Truth was my friend that day. No one cared about my opinion, what I thought had happened, or my take on people's motives. The attorney tried to lead me in those directions. I stuck with truth.

The Marine colonel played by Jack Nicholson in *A Few Good Men* did not, at first, stick with truth. The young attorney knew it, and ultimately the real truth came out.

Many of us have been guilty of manipulating the truth as well. In fact at a dinner this week, without using the word "truth" a single time, those of us there talked about people who intentionally create their own truth, an alternate reality.

The people we were talking about: golfers. Not all golfers by a long shot, but a particular group of golfers known pejoratively as "sandbaggers."

Golfers who play in competitions establish a handicap by turning in their golf scores to a handicap committee. In return, the committee gives the golfer a handicap -- a number. Skilled golfers get lower numbers, and those numbers are intended to level the playing field so that skilled and unskilled golfers can compete against each other. The handicap evens things out.

Results

Some golfers, however, say their golf scores were higher than they really were. Or they turn in high scores and not low scores. Both are a form of "not telling the truth," so the handicap they are assigned is also a lie.

When they enter a competition with that handicap number, they have a big advantage. And they often leave the tournament with a trophy and a bad reputation.

That is really no different than telling the government you made less money than you did.

Some people think we are supposed to cheat on our taxes (we aren't), but cheating in the world of golf is looked down upon both widely and deeply.

Sandbaggers are often kicked out of tournaments and even banned from future competitions. Lying has consequences.

The colonel was wrong

People in general *can* handle the truth. Sometime speaking the truth or hearing the truth can be painful, especially when the truth reveals a lie that has been told.

The colonel was the one who could not handle the truth, because it uncovered his own biased version of events.

Over the centuries people have created different theories of truth, always in an attempt to negate the idea that truth is that which corresponds with reality or facts. These theories get more or less attention based on culture, and today's culture is no exception.

In most of these theories, beliefs take the place of reality and facts, and there is a lot of that going around.

At its most basic, people say "If I believe it is true, that makes it true."

No, it doesn't. But more and more people are being misled by it.

I'll write more about that next week, but for now I'll leave you with a line from philosopher Mortimer J. Adler.

He said that two men in a rowboat approaching a bend in the river who firmly believe the waterfall is a mile away when in fact it is just around the corner still die.

Seek truth. Embrace truth. Do good. It's in you.

Chapter 33

Things Sherlock and God See That We Don't

Detective stories, whether in books or on TV or in a movie, attract a lot of us.

I think part of the reason is because we love puzzles, and a good mystery or detective story is a delightful kind of puzzle. We try to figure out what the lead character has figured out (or will), and then we say, "Of course!" when we see it.

From *Monk*, one of my all time favorites, to *Miss Marple*, to the fairly new *Elsbeth*, the lead character is often a little bit "different." Writers have always made them that way.

Maybe that helps us know why we can't do what they can do. At the heart of them all, though, is that they see things we don't.

The Mentalist was the same, and so was *Psych*. The master of them all, of course, and the detective to which all detectives aspire, was *Sherlock Holmes*.

Created by Sir Arthur Conan Doyle, Mr. Holmes first appeared to the public in 1887. Eventually he was featured in four novels and 56 short stories. So intrigued are we by the "consulting detective" that screen adaptations of his story continue to be written today.

The first part of the magic of Holmes is his ability to notice small details that are important to the case. Actually, that is also the initial magic of Monk, of Patrick Jane ("the mentalist"), and of Elsbeth Tascioni.

The second part of the magic, and the part most of us think we could rise to, is putting all that information together to reach a logical and accurate conclusion.

Here is what's different about Sherlock Holmes, us, and someone even better than Holmes — God.

Details...

"I noticed, Watson, a slight smudge on the cuff of the the fellow who just stopped us to ask the time," said Holmes. "No doubt you saw it as well and know that it was oil. But are you aware that it was actually synthetic oil?"

"That's astonishing!" answered Watson. "I did not know synthetic oil had been produced."

"It hasn't," said Holmes. "It is perhaps 50 years away. But when it is made it will be used in pendulum clocks. As our fellow tipped his cap to thank us, his cuff came within a few inches of my face and I smelled the chemical mixture. Obviously the man is a clock maker from the future. He can't be the murderer, because he wasn't here yesterday."

See how simple it is? Observe, understand, reason, conclude.

By contrast, here is how we do it.

"Did you guys notice that fellow has a Jewish name? He's probably pro-Israel, so we hate him."

Notice, conclude, opine.

We notice some things, but not because we are observant. We are actively looking for things that support our opinions. When we find them we eat them up so that our opinions get stronger and less vulnerable.

There is a well known account in the Bible of a fellow who did exactly that. His name — or actually his title — was Pharaoh.

Oh yeah?

Imagine this historical event as a boxing match.

In this corner, former adopted grandson of a former Pharaoh, most recently a shepherd, 80-year-old Moses! He is assisted by his older brother Aaron, who is carrying a stick.

And in this corner, ruler of all of Egypt and one of the most powerful men in the world, Pharaoh! He is assisted by several magicians and a gigantic army.

The match began because Moses showed up in Egypt, where he had been wanted for murder, and demanded that Pharaoh let all the Hebrew people (they were enslaved) go. Since there were more than a half-million of them, that would have affected the economy in a big way. Pharaoh said no.

Round 1: God, through Moses and Aaron, turned all the water in the Nile river — and even water in stone pots — into blood. Yuck! Pharaoh's magicians did something very similar, so the answer was still no.

This went on for a total of 10 plagues on Egypt. Those included frogs, gnats (the magicians couldn't do that and told Pharaoh to throw in the towel), and darkness.

Every time, though, Pharaoh's heart was made harder instead of softer.

After the 10th plague, the death of the firstborn in every household, including Pharaoh's, the Hebrew people were finally released.

But Pharaoh's heart was still hard. You may know he pursued the Hebrews and in the process was drowned, along with much of his army, in the Red Sea.

There was no reasoning with Pharaoh. Nor is there with many today who will not listen to even the strongest evidence.

Their minds are made up, and their hearts are turning — or have turned — to stone.

The heart of the matter

Sherlock Holmes used a form of reasoning called *deductive reasoning*. That is also called *deduction*, because in it specific conclusions are formed from general premises. If the premises are correct, deductive reasoning can never be wrong.

Inductive reasoning, on the other hand, is forming general theories from specific observations, and while helpful it is often wrong.

A career criminal who says, "My people will get me out of jail because they always have" is using inductive reasoning. He could be right or he could be wrong. Inductive reasoning is used in things like climate change. We predict the future based on some part of the past.

So what does God see that we don't? What does he see clearly that even Sherlock Holmes might miss?

He sees our heart. Is our heart open and pliant, or is it closed and rigid?

God saw Pharaoh's heart and knew that reasoning with him would make his heart harder. You know people like that, but the real question is, are *you* a person like that?

If we truly want to do good to all of mankind, we need to look less at externals and much more at hearts, including our own.

We will never detect like Holmes, and we will never see hearts as well as God sees them, but we can learn to observe.

Do good. It's in you! And you don't even need a magnifying glass.

Chapter 34

Listen To This...

I t seems to me there is a trend toward listening these days, because podcasts are a big deal.

My songwriting partner, Gary, and I had one about 25 years ago, when they were trending but not trendy. But with newer and better technology, podcasts are both easier to produce and access. It's unlikely they'll every replace blogs, though, which are even easier to produce.

Communicating audibly obviously predates any system of writing. The oldest writing discovered, estimated from around 35,000 BC, was on what might have been a coffee mug. No one is 100% sure, but scholars believe it translates to "World's Best Dad."

The great thing about that sentence, and about the written word in general, is that you can reread it and laugh (or groan) one more time.

But my goal here is not to pit the spoken word against the written word. I love writing, but the spoken word wins that battle if for no other reason than this famous (written) passage:

"And God said, "Let there be light," and there was light." (Genesis

1:3) In fact, according to Genesis, God spoke the whole world into existence.

To add to the gravitas and majesty and mystery of all this, John the Apostle wrote, "In the beginning was the Word, and the Word was with God and the Word was God.... All things were made through him." The Word turns out to be Jesus, whose birth we celebrated a few weeks ago.

So yeah (as they say these days), the spoken word wins.

Speaking and writing are both powerful in their own way, but one thing I love is the written recording of spoken words. And I'm not talking about podcasts, I'm talking about speeches.

"I have a dream today."

A few days after the publication of these written words, America will celebrate the birthday of Martin Luther King Jr.

When it was decided that there should be a national holiday in his honor, I was initially a skeptic. I liked King just fine, but did he deserve a holiday like Washington and Lincoln?

No longer a skeptic, I'm glad we remember King the way we do. I just wish we remembered more of his speech than "I have a dream." Perhaps we could remember, for instance, what the dream was about.

Just before writing this article, I read again the entire speech that King delivered that day. I noticed some things you might find interesting.

First, more than 250,000 people were there to hear the speech in person. That is far more than I ever pictured. The speech was delivered on the steps of the Lincoln Memorial in Washington D.C. on August 28, 1963. This was the culmination of a civil rights march, and the location was no accident.

The Lincoln Memorial was the perfect setting. King knew that.

What also struck me as I reread the speech was the opening line:

"Five score years ago, a great American, in whose symbolic shadow we stand today, signed the Emancipation Proclamation."

Did you catch that "Five score years ago" phrase? It is clearly a reference to Lincoln's own Gettysburg Address, another speech that changed the world, which began "Four score and seven years ago...."

King's entire speech is composed of simple words spoken with power and conviction. He drew two great pictures from the Bible. *"Until justice rolls down like waters, and righteousness like a mighty stream"* is from Amos.

(I have a dream that) *one day every valley shall be exalted and every hill and mountain shall be made low, the rough places will be made plain and the crooked places will be made straight, and the glory of the Lord shall be revealed and all flesh shall see it together...*

is from Isaiah.

More than talk

In 1964, the year following his most famous speech, Martin Luther King Jr. was awarded the Nobel Peace Prize for his fight against racial inequality. The list of awards he received for his work is long, and will continue to grow.

He was not only eloquent, he was intelligent. He earned a PhD in Theology, he wrote, he led, and he influenced millions.

But many of us remember him for his powerful oratory, especially the "I have a dream" speech.

That speech can make your heart beat faster as you listen to him deliver it.

"I've seen the promised land" is a speech that will make your spine tingle -- partly because of the words and partly because of the timing.

Delivered on April 3, 1968, in Memphis, Tennessee, King opened that speech with a story from 1960. He was in New York City autographing copies of his first book. As he was signing, he heard a woman ask if he was Martin Luther King.

While looking down he said he was, and "the next minute I felt something beating on my chest."

The woman (he describes her as a "demented black woman") had stabbed him. It was the first attempt on his life, and it came very close to succeeding -- the tip of the blade was on the edge of his aorta. The New York Times reported that "if he had sneezed, he could have died."

He said in this speech he was glad he didn't sneeze, because in the past eight years a lot of progress had been made. Then he finished with this:

But it doesn't matter with me now. Because I've been to the mountaintop. And I don't mind. Like anybody, I would like to live a long life... but I'm not concerned about that now. I just want to do God's will. And he's allowed me to go up to the mountain. And I've looked over. And I've seen the promised land.

I may not get there with you. But I want you to know tonight, that we as a people will get to the promised land. And I'm happy, tonight. I'm not worried about anything. I'm not fearing any man. Mine eyes have seen the glory of the coming of the Lord.

The very next morning, King was assassinated.

May his words and his work inspire us all to do good.

Chapter 35

"Did we win?"

Do you remember Damar Hamlin? In case you don't, allow me to tell you about him.

Damar is a professional football player, a safety for the Buffalo Bills, and he suffered cardiac arrest on the field in early 2023. It was the first quarter of a nationally televised game against the Cincinnati Bengals. Hamlin was involved in a tackle and appeared to take a blow to the chest.

The 24 year old got up from the ground, took a couple of steps, then collapsed. Team personnel were with him immediately, and an ambulance was brought onto the field. Denny Kellington, Bills Assistant Athletic Trainer, performed CPR and likely saved Hamlin's life. Damar was taken to the University of Cincinnati Medical Center, where he received outstanding care.

Reports a few days later said he was awake and improving. His first communication -- written, because he had a breathing tube -- was, "Did we win?" For a lot of reasons, that made the doctors smile.

The game was actually suspended, which was appropriate, and late Thursday evening it was cancelled. That has interesting implications for the playoffs.

But what is far more important to me is the reaction of football players, sportscasters, other athletes, and everyday people to what happened on the field Monday.

Prayer?

A picture of something that happened after the play was posted on Twitter by Robert Griffin III, a very famous football player (Heisman Trophy, All Pro QB, etc.). He wrote "Please don't share the video of the Damar Hamlin play. Share this because we are all praying for him and his family."

What he asked everyone to share is a picture from the Buffalo Bills organization. It shows players and personnel from both teams spontaneously gathered at mid-field and praying for Damar Hamlin after the ambulance took him.

All of us have heard the standard phrase "thoughts and prayers," which is directly related to "How are you?" and "I'm good" in depth of meaning. They are placeholders, throw away words we speak out of habit, rarely out of our hearts.

Many newscasters used the "thoughts and prayers" phrase, but one who did not embrace it was Dan Orlovsky.

Dan is a former NFL quarterback who is now a sportscaster with ESPN. During a broadcast, with two other sportscasters on the set with him, he said, "Maybe this is not the right thing to do, but it's on my heart and I want to pray for him right now."

He said he was going to close his eyes and bow his head and pray, and he did.

Many people who were watching that broadcast recorded it and tweeted it. Millions of people have now watched it, and the response has been overwhelmingly encouraging and thankful.

In case you haven't seen it, you can see Franklin Graham's retweet of it on X.

Is this OK?

There are a number of things people do in private that should only be done in private. I know you can name several.

Increasingly a faction of society has added prayer to that list. Never mind that prayer has been done in public since people began talking to God. Forget that sessions of Congress begin with prayer. Ignore the fact that the inauguration of a United States president includes prayer.

The goal, it seems, is to remove God from the public picture.

That's why former high school football coach Joe Kennedy eventually found himself in the Supreme Court of the United States. Famously, now, the Bremerton High coach would go out to the middle of the field after a game and pray. Eventually some students decided to join him, and you probably know the rest.

His first prayer on the Bremerton High field was in 2008, and the case was decided in his favor by the Supreme Court in 2022. Fourteen years from that first prayer to the courts approving his actons.

And in about fourteen minutes on the Monday night of Damar Hamilton's collapse, dozens of people decided that it was OK to pray in public on a football field.

Yes, I know the complaint against Coach Kennedy was that his actions might give the impression that the school endorsed and even encouraged prayer. I know this is not high school. But both the Hamlin game and the Bremerton High School games are football, a potentially dangerous sport.

I won't dive into that any deeper here. What I will say is that the hearts of people responded to the near death of Damar Hamlin the way hearts respond, and that is good.

Team

The Buffalo Bills organization has been all over this. They said publicly they believe in prayer. Their response, and the response of the NFL, has been beautiful.

You might expect that from Hamlin's team, but it has gone beyond that. The Buffalo Hockey team all donned jerseys with Hamlin's number -- 3 -- on them.

NBA teams and players poured out support for Damar. Public buildings changed their lights to blue -- the color of the Buffalo Bills -- to honor Hamlin.

Many on Twitter changed their profile picture from themselves to a meme saying "Pray for Damar - 3," including the Buffalo Bills themselves.

When the good news was announced that Damar was awake and that it appeared that he was neurologically intact, the reactions were on point.

Bills head coach Sean McDermott said, "Glory to God for his keeping Damar and his family in the palm of his hand over the last couple of days, and for his healing power."

Damar's GoFundMe account raising money for kids has received more than $7,000,000 in donations this week! My favorite was a $19,203 donation from the Chicago Bears. 1920 is the year the Bears were founded, and 3 is Damar's number. Connection.

Did we win?

One of his doctors answered that question later with, "Yes, Damar. You've won the game of life."

And in no small way, so have we all. Millions of people prayed unselfishly. Thousands of people gave money. Cincinnati school children sent get well cards.

"Did we win?"

We came together for something outside ourselves.
Can we keep doing that?
Let's continue to do good. It is obviously in us.

Chapter 36

Making Time

One of my occasional pastimes is crossword puzzles. I was solving one the other day that had a couple of clues dealing with climate change. So when I found a clue that said, "Non-renewable resource" my mind went to the usual villains du jour.

It turned out, though, that the answer was *time*. Non-renewable is certainly how it feels. We never seem to have enough time, and we can't make any more of it.

Or can we?

Time, you may know, is a distinctly human element. Animals don't measure it and God is, as C. S. Lewis puts it, "outside of time." The apostle Peter said, "But you must not forget this one thing, dear friends: A day is like a thousand years to the Lord, and a thousand years is like a day."

So only we humans measure it, think about it, and (too often) are enslaved by it.

You may wonder, if you take the time to think about it, where this whole idea of time came from. You may also wonder why only people care about time. Another time I'll answer the second question, but for now let's answer the first.

Where is the sun?

Genesis chapter 1 has it like this:

Then God said, "Let there be light," and there was light. And God saw that the light was good. Then he separated the light from the darkness. God called the light "day" and the darkness "night."

And evening passed and morning came, marking the first day.

And thus time was created, separated into day and night. But where is the sun? It is not the light.

Keep reading and you find:

Then God said, "Let lights appear in the sky to separate the day from the night. Let them be signs to mark the seasons, days, and years. Let these lights in the sky shine down on the earth." And that is what happened. God made two great lights—the larger one to govern the day, and the smaller one to govern the night. He also made the stars. God set these lights in the sky to light the earth, to govern the day and night, and to separate the light from the darkness. And God saw that it was good.

And evening passed and morning came, marking the fourth day.

Personally I think it is very cool that day and night existed before the sun and moon, but that the sun and moon "mark the seasons, days and years."

Of course you may not think God did any of that, but you still measure your life by the light and the dark, as do we all.

Getting outside of time

In Hawaii, and in some other tropical climes around the world, you will find the concept of "island time." My interpretation of that is, *when it happens, it happens.*

Much of the rest of the world demands a closer accounting of every second of every minute of every hour. Happily, those who live on island time are more often *outside of time* than those who are held captive by every minute.

All of us have experienced being outside of time. It might have happened to you while climbing a mountain or floating in the ocean. You may have gone outside of time while reading a book or having a conversation with a very good friend. Perhaps you were just lost in thought, or in a project, and time passed without you knowing it.

Good for you!

You probably didn't get to that "a thousand years is like a day" level, but you know the feeling. All you are really doing is being free from the shackles of time while using it beneficially.

I experienced that this week when I was helping my friend Jimmy with his golf game. He was working hard and making good progress. No one watching could say which of us was enjoying it more. For the most part, though, we were unaware of time passing. And it was good.

Does getting outside of time increase the objective amount of time you have? It does not add hours to the day, but it might add days — or even years — to your life.

Give your time away

Some psychologists and philosophers have noticed the positive effect of giving time to others. Though you cannot create more "real" time, giving time to others will make you feel as though you can.

This same thing is true for almost everything we have to give, from money to love. It is definitely true with time. Hold it tightly for your own use and it will become heavy and cruel. Give it away, especially to those who need your time, and it will become light and good.

Consider the following uses of your time and think about how they impacted you.

First, spending an hour or more on social media. Reading, post-ing, commenting, etc. Second, spending that same time on other people by helping them or having them help you.

Many of us have spent time on social media and then felt like we "wasted" it. That never makes us feel better about ourselves.

And all of us have given time to someone else and known it was a very good thing to do.

Finding the time

As I've grown in my ability to give away time and get outside of time, I have also found more time. Where? In places where I once spent it with little or no benefit.

I virtually never watch the news. My social media accounts are visited so rarely I don't remember my passwords. The TV I watch is limited.

But my goal is not to "manage" my time, my goal is to be a wise steward of the gift of time. And those who are wise stewards receive more.

Get outside of time. Give your time away. Be a wise steward of time. If we do those things with time, we might just make more of it.

Besides, those are all beautiful ways to do good.

Chapter 37

What Do You Know? (And what will you do with it?)

E verybody knows something. I know some things. My wife knows other things. Expand that list to our families and friends, and together we know far more. One piece of knowledge we share is who to call about things we don't know about.

Is it a good thing that in these days we turn to a keyboard with crumbs in it and a light emitting screen instead of a friend? (Quick, search for "how do I clean my keyboard." And stop eating at your desk.) Do we talk to Alexa and Siri more than we talk to a person who actually cares about us?

But I digress. My question for all of us today is: now that we know stuff, what do we do with it?

Test, tease, tempt

Testing your knowledge can be a lot of fun. It can also be lucrative.

The fun part for me includes doing crossword puzzles and watching *Jeopardy!*. In fact the appeal of both of those things is finding out we actually know things, and that there is still much to learn.

To test your knowledge and also make a little money, try to become a contestant on *Jeopardy!*. It is possible to become rich and famous that way. You can also test your crossword knowledge and ability in contests -- with prize money!

If you know something no one else knows, like the formula that became Original Coke, you can tease the world with it. Colonel Sanders did that with his Original Recipe (11 herbs and spices) chicken. Bush's Best Beans did it, too, although their dog, Duke, tried hard to sell that formula.

And of course you can tempt others with some special knowledge. That can be as innocent as a sideshow at a county fair or as insidious as insider trading.

Sell it

Many people who have learned some things well sell that knowledge. Consultants, lawyers, and computer programmers all do that. So do professional teachers of all kinds, from college profs to pickleball pros.

People also sell their knowledge by making videos and putting them on YouTube. Viewers don't pay them directly, of course. They are paid by those advertisers you mostly ignore when you watch videos.

Out of curiosity I researched most watched videos, etc., on social media. Entertainment makes the most money. Education? Pretty much not there. Unless you combine it with some entertainment.

Vocal coach Cheryl Porter does that and has more than 10,000,000 subscribers on YouTube. That puts her slightly behind the entertainment leader MrBeast and his 245,000,000 subscribers. He's fun, but she is making the world sound better.

Speaking of selling information, automobile manufacturers have been collecting data about the driving habits of individual people and selling that.

They've been using a connected service like OnStar to "watch" how the owners drive. Then they sell that data to LexisNexis. That company analyzes the data, gives each driver a score, and sells that to insurance companies which then adjust people's individual insurance rates.

As far as I know they haven't lowered anyone's rates. Raised them? Yes. One driver, a customer of his insurance company for 40 years with no accidents or incidents, had his rate doubled based on that data.

Who knew your driving habits were worth so much?

More info about you

To say that Google has a lot of data about you is an understatement. They have pages and pages and pages -- books, perhaps -- of data about you.

That is not a secret. Google is in the data business, not the search business, not the video business, and not the email business.

And if you want to know what they know about you they'll show you. Actually you can go to your account and download a file of everything they have on you. So I did that. The compressed file was almost 1 GB.

It's kind of fun looking at the things I had searched for on YouTube. They mostly fell into two categories: how to repair things around the house and how to swing a golf club.

But the best find for me was listening to a few voice mails (I used to have a Google phone number) from my mother-in-law. She passed away almost a decade ago, but we were great pals and it made me smile to hear her voice again.

In general, though, I spent too much time going through all of that information. Kind of like spending too much time on YouTube watching golf swings.

Give it away

One thing you can do with what you know is give it away, and I'm a pretty big fan of doing that.

If you want information on how to play golf, all you have to do is wander over to a public driving range and start swinging. The worse you are, the more likely it is that people will stop to help you. I love that about golfers. Please note that what they tell you may be totally wrong, but they are sharing.

The same can be true in almost any endeavor. People really do want to help. I'll bet that includes you.

So how are you giving away -- or sharing, if you like that better -- your knowledge? Just as you are occasionally looking for someone to help you with something, start looking for people you can help using the things you know.

For the last two years I have volunteered to teach a class on leadership to student athletes at Grand Canyon University. They don't get credit and I don't get paid, but it's a joy for us all. What and whom and where could you teach?

One special way to share your knowledge is by mentoring. I have a retired friend who is intentional about finding mentees and working with them. They are learning a lot from what he gives them. Maybe you could do that.

Of all the things we possess, what we know is extraordinarily precious. We can give it away over and over and still keep it.

And in both using it and sharing it, we can do an amazing amount of good.

Do good. It's in you!

Chapter 38

Has the Search for Truth Been Abandoned?

There once was a man -- a long, long time ago -- named Diogenes.

There could have been more than one, as I think of it, but the Diogenes (di-ah'-jin-eze) we remember lived around 300 to 400 years before Christ. He was witty, wise, and a great teacher.

For much of his life, Diogenes lived in Athens. It is said that he would walk about the city in broad daylight while carrying a lighted lantern. When asked what he was doing, he would reply, "I am looking for a man." (Anyone who has not been corrupted by the world.)

Many have his answer as, "I am looking for an honest man." That would have fit his philosophy and been just as hard to find.

His philosophy was known as Cynicism. In fact he is often called Diogenes the Cynic.

Cynicism favored courage over fortune, reason over passion, and (most important) nature over convention. In other words, live a natural life, not how the world tells you to live.

You can bet that no Cynic would have an account on TikTok. Or any kind of social-media, for that matter. They would also not seek wealth or worldly goods. Living as simply as possible was the goal, and Diogenes modeled that.

Still, he was a seeker of wisdom and most definitely a seeker of truth.

The search is on!

Everyone who seeks wisdom, knowledge, and truth is a philosopher. I'm guessing that includes you, though you may never have thought of yourself as a philosopher. First, let's establish that you are a seeker. Think for just a moment of all the things you have looked for just this week.

In the last day (mostly in the last few hours), I have personally searched for:

- a tax return from a previous year
- an attorney who specializes in business and corporate law
- a logo for a company so I could create a small sign
- a TED talk with content that is important for this article
- a comment on that TED talk
- the fastest way to get from a meeting in one town to a meeting in another town

Mundane? Absolutely! Most of what we seek is not exciting or even interesting, especially out of context. So here are other things I find myself seeking:

- a perfect golf swing
- my phone
- the best pizza within two miles of my home
- a television show that will make me smile, laugh occasionally, think a little, and not be offensive

- pancakes that are crispy on the outside and fluffy on the inside
- someone with integrity to lead the free world

My point is that whether it is exciting or not, much of our time is spent looking for something. Truth is one of those things I am always on the lookout for. Always.

Seek and you will find

The best selling book of all time has a lot to say about seeking. If you've read it, or even if you've heard it quoted, you might know: *Seek and you will find.* That phrase is one of three that come together. The other two are "knock and the door will be opened," and "ask and it will be given." (The actual order, which makes no difference, is ask, seek, knock.)

One of the fun things about ask, seek, knock is this. All of those verbs are in a particular Greek tense that implies continuous action. That means we should read it like this: *ask and keep on asking, seek and keep on seeking, knock and keep on knocking.* There is no promise of an immediate payoff for our one-time efforts. Sorry.

Of course if we really want something, what difficulty is there in keeping on?

When your 5 year old child or grandchild wants something and you say no, do they simply say "OK" and walk away? Ha!

If you really are trying to find something, you will seek it with thought, energy, and your best sleuthing skills.

In my home office, the top of my desk is a place where even a small dog might get lost.

So when I am looking for some particular paper, or a receipt, or a book I've pulled off the shelf, I always suspect *the desk.* But I don't look there first, because it is too hard. I look on the floor and in various chairs -- even in other rooms. Finally I get to the desktop, and I *seek.*

When my wife gets home she will look at my uncluttered desk top and ask, "What did you lose?"

Do I look that diligently for the truth? Or, like many people today, do I simply look for someone who agrees with me?

That lady in the TED Talk

Her name is Katherine Maher. She is not related to the comedian and talk show host Bill Maher. He even said he kind of wished she pronounced her name differently.

Ms. Maher was once the CEO of The Wikimedia Foundation, which is the host of Wikipedia, which is the seventh most visited website in the world. In 2022 she gave a TED Talk, and in it said:

"Our reverence for the truth might be a distraction that is getting in the way of finding common ground and getting things done. That is not to say that the truth doesn't exist or to say that the truth isn't important. Clearly the search for the truth has led us to do great things...."

So, stop seeking truth and start seeking common ground? I thought truth *was* common ground.

Commentator Jonah Goldberg recently wrote that we now live in a philodoxical age rather than a philosophical age. That means we now love *opinion* rather than *wisdom* or truth. He is right, and he knows it will only get worse.

How do we reverse it?

Seek truth, even if it is hard to find. Let's get our lanterns out and light them and hit the streets. Truth is still out there, and so are truth-tellers.

Do good! It's in you.

Chapter 39

The Advantages of Time Travel

Back *To The Future* was one of those delightful movies with a great cast, a solid story, likeable characters, and a bad guy named Biff.

The good guy wins, which is what viewers want, but the writers were savvy enough to create an opening for a sequel. That came four years later, with another coming one year after that.

Michael J. Fox was the star, along with the most excellent Christopher Lloyd. But perhaps the most compelling character in the series was a time-traveling DeLorean automobile.

If you're a fan of *Back To The Future*, you may remember that it required 1.21 gigawatts (GW) of electricity to power the DeLorean. If you happen to be an energy nerd -- or just curious — do a web search to find out how much 1 GW is. The solar panels would not fit on your roof.

If you traveled back in time in the western world, you would find a book on time travel that was written in 1733. *Memoirs of the Twentieth Century* may in fact be the first book in the genre.

Other time travel stories include *Rip Van Winkle,* and *A*

Christmas Carol (Scrooge, et al). Of course *Back To The Future* is far from being either the first or last time travel movie.

Although it would be fun, you don't need a DeLorean to travel to and learn about the past. That's good, because can you imagine the electric bill for charging one of those puppies?

There are two ways to travel back in time. One way is in your mind. The other is through books, including the Bible. It talks about the past *and* the future.

Joseph

It occurred to me recently that some of the most recognized names in the Bible start with J.

Jesus, Judas, and Job are names many people know. Jesus is, well, Jesus. Top of the list. Superstar. Judas is known for betraying Jesus, and Job is known for his amazing patience.

One other J person you might have heard of, even if you've never read the Bible, is Joseph. He was the guy with "the amazing technicolor dreamcoat." (Fun musical, but I think the book is better.)

Joseph, so you know this part of his story, saved the nation of Egypt from starvation. He did that by interpreting a dream for Pharaoh (king of Egypt) that foretold seven years of plenty followed by seven years of famine. Joseph was then put in charge of making sure the country and its people survived all 14 years. He succeeded.

Because of all that, Joseph was revered in Egypt. But time passed. Joseph and his sons died. Pharaoh died, and the Pharaoh after him, and other Pharaohs as well.

Then the Bible says, "Now there arose a new king over Egypt, who did not know Joseph."

(It's too bad Tim Rice and Andrew Lloyd Webber weren't around then to write the musical and help keep Joseph's name alive.)

That particular Pharaoh was not a good man, and he later drowned in the Red Sea. But it seems to me that the first flaw we find in his character is that he was not a time traveler. He didn't learn from the past.

It's about now

To say there is a lot going on in the world today would be like saying a 1 gigawatt light bulb would be bright. Just as that would be blinding, our information flow is overwhelming. News is big business. People want to know, and media companies give us all that and more. We are flooded with information.

And of course most of it is bad news.

To demonstrate how burdensome all this is, think about the sense of relief you feel when you read a news story that is good.

And when there isn't any new bad news, old bad news gets repeated.

Think of a recent news story. How many times have you heard it? The media keeps our attention in the now by doing that. Rehash the football game or golf tournament if you enjoy that. Rehashing the news, though, is almost always a poor use of our time.

Why? Because living only in the now keeps us from traveling in time. We use little to no time dreaming about the future or learning from the past. Of course it isn't just the media. The very real demands of "now" are often important, but "now" is always better with occasional visits to the future and the past.

Only humans, as far as we know, can time travel. We can imagine things in the future and then decide if we want to go there, and how.

We can look back at the past and learn from the greats about how they accomplished things. And we can understand mistakes from the past (including our own) and not repeat them in the now.

These are amazing gifts. We should embrace them, practice them, and reap the benefits.

See into the future

We can, as I once wrote in a lyric, see into the future. We do that by looking into the eyes and hearts of the next couple of generations. But we should not *live* in the future, nor should we dwell in the past.

The mistake of younger people -- Arthur Brooks says his MBA students do this -- is to think mostly about the future. As a result, they miss the gift of the present.

The mistake some older people make is spending too much time in the past. Partly that happens because older people recall many times of great joy. Reliving those is not bad. Living in the past, though, is not good.

Time travel is something we all should do intentionally. Just don't get stuck in the past, like Michael J. Fox almost did in *Back To The Future*, and don't get lost in the future and forget to enjoy the journey that gets you there.

And no matter where you travel in time, always do good. It's in you.

Chapter 40

Five Resolutions for Any New Year

This article about resolutions is from 2021 but is still one of my favorites. The great thing to remember is this: you don't have to wait for January — you can start a new year any day you like and still call them "New Year's Resolutions."

Making New Year's Resolutions is not always easy, but I'm here for you. My suggestions for your list will not be, shall we say, standard fare. But we'll start with one that is -- the perennial Number 1: ***Lose weight/exercise more***.

That is a resolution many Americans could use. In fact Healthline noted way back in June, 2020, that 36.5% of the people in the United States were obese, and another 32.5% were overweight.

Since then we've had Thanksgiving and Christmas, one of the easiest times of the year to gain weight. (Ask me how I know.)

Exercise is really good for you. Do it and you will gain energy, sleep better (also good for you), drink more water (ditto), and feel better about yourself.

The very best exercise for losing weight is called the push-away, and it can be done two different ways. You can push the plate away, or you can push your chair away from the table. Both work.

Lose weight/exercise more is a great resolution, and for 69% of us it deserves to be at the top of the list. It is also a terrific way to do good. So write it down and get after it. I'm with you!

Now for the rest of your list

As for the rest of your list, allow me to suggest a few resolutions that are a little out of the norm.

Whether you use these or not, make sure at least part of the focus -- if not the major focus -- of each resolution is on other people. Besides, it seems wrong to go from one of the most giving and caring times in the year to one of the most self-centered, all in a matter of days.

In fact your second resolution might be: ***Think more about others***. If you really do that, your thoughts will turn into words and your words will turn into actions. The bottom line is that if you think more about others you will eventually do more for others.

Here's a cool thing about this resolution. *The worse your life is, the more helpful it is to you to think about others.*

I can hear some of you saying, "Whaaaat?" But it's true. Doctors, psychologists, and my own experiences verify that thinking of others is good for your physical and mental health.

And if your life is great, then definitely stop bragging to yourself about yourself and think of others. Use some of those blessings to do good, and your life will be even better.

Number 3

My next suggestion for 2021: ***Use my gifts for the benefit of others***.

What does that mean? If you can sing, join the church choir so people can hear your voice. Or go to a karaoke bar, but let people enjoy your gift. If you are great at business, find a startup or a struggling business and help them. For free. Maybe you've been given a great smile. Use it when you check out at a store. (Note: this works even if you are wearing a mask due to COVID. Your eyes smile too.)

How does smiling help you? First of all, people will smile back, and that's fun. Or they may be totally startled, and the look on their face will still be fun. Second, your outward smile will creep into your own body and make you feel good, too. Third, smiles spread even faster than a virus. Be a superspreader!

In fact using any gift in a good way will guarantee you two things. First, you'll get better at whatever your gift is. Second, the Giver of those gifts will be pleased and will give you more gifts.

Number 4

There may be a little bit of bias in this one, but I still like it. **Read more books and watch less TV**.

Here's the thing: reading a book is much more active than watching a show. There are many excellent movies, and even quite a few good TV shows, but most of the best movies started life as a book. And the book is always better.

Do you love *The Lord of the Rings*? You should read the books, starting with *The Hobbit*. Are you a fan of Jordan Peterson on YouTube? Read his book, *12 Rules for Life*. Do you like movies that have a good moral lesson? Read the Bible. *The Greatest Game Ever Played* is an excellent golf movie. The book is richer by far.

Of course you can watch a movie in less time than it takes to read a book, but the book will stay in you longer. I love the experience of a great movie in a great theater, and still remember some of those from years ago. I'm not knocking movies and TV, but I am saying that books are better for you, and that makes you better for others.

Number 5

Maybe this should really be number one, but I'm going to believe that we will keep all our resolutions with equal integrity. At least that's our intent, right?

Anyway, here's one you won't find on many lists. It's an old church hymn (1896) that has lasted, and when people start talking about resolutions this always comes to my mind. I don't know how many times I sang this in church, but it wasn't the repetition that made it stick, it was the message. It starts with lines that are applicable to everyone.

I am resolved no longer to linger,
Charmed by the world's delight,
Things that are higher, things that are nobler,
These have allured my sight.

Resolve to not be charmed (and led) by the world's delight. **Look for things that are higher, things that are nobler, and focus on those**.

If you are a minimalist, or just very efficient, here's your one resolution: ***I resolve to do good all year***.

Good for you.

Acknowledgments

In 1998 Kim Basinger was receiving an Academy Award for Best Supporting Actress in a Feature Film. Because it was one of the big awards, it was near the end of the show. Throughout the evening, recipients had stepped forward with joy to collect their statuette and say "Thank you" to everyone they could think of. Some had notes, but at least one came back to add another name.

When Ms. Basinger was handed the Oscar, she smiled, turned to the audience and said, "I just want to thank everyone I've ever met in my entire life."

I get that, but in this particular case I'm going to thank everyone who has ever read anything I've ever written, most of whom I've never met.

I want to thank Erik and John and Judy and Bill for making suggestions regarding which articles should "definitely" be included in this book. And I also want to thank Erik for his subtitle suggestion that led me immediately to the one we used.

Though he passed away before I started Do Good U, I often think of my friend Jeff Hopper, the original editor of the Links Players International daily devotional. He both encouraged me as a writer and helped me "write tighter."

Judy, my wife, has acted throughout all of my writings — through many years and many forms of writing — as my chief proofreader and occasional editor. And she has often carried out those tasks long after she would rather have been asleep. Her work is a blessing for us all.

Mostly, and with genuine gratitude, my thanks goes to the Giver of all gifts, God, for giving me a love for words and the ability to use them in writing.

And a very special *thank you* for reading this book. May it bring good into your life that you can bring into the world.

About the Author

Lewis Greer, the founder and CEO of Do Good University, Inc., is a lifelong learner, teacher, writer, and leader. He has worked in a wide variety of fields, from ministry to music and from tennis to tech, and currently serves as the Arizona director of Links Players International.

This is his third non-fiction book. He has also written the book and lyrics for a musical on the life of Jesus, as well as the lyrics for many songs.

Lewis and his wife, Judy, reside in the Valley of the Sun.

About Do Good U

With a focus on leadership and culture, Do Good U helps guide companies and schools to more profitability, stronger teams, and work/school experiences that create loyalty and productivity.

Using time tested (thousands of years) techniques, we help both staff and students find and fulfill a purpose that transcends the day-to-day so they can bring more good into the world.

www.ingramcontent.com/pod-product-compliance
Lightning Source LLC
Chambersburg PA
CBHW052046090426
42739CB00010B/2063